COPY ~~RIGHT~~

TABLE OF CONTENTS

I dedicate this book to my family: Jan, Jasmine & Joel, Sunday & Zion, Keziah & James, Nathan, Rowan

I want to express my heartfelt thanks to the five wonderful people who spent time editing the manuscript: Bridget Trayling, Darrell Cocup, Jan Isherwood, Jenny Reid, Ali Perry. I so appreciate your time and input!

FORWARD BY CRAIG COONEY

When I think of Alan Kilpatrick, the following verse from Jeremiah comes to mind:

"See, today I appoint you over nations and kingdoms to uproot and tear down, to destroy and overthrow, to build and to plant." (Jeremiah 1:10)

Alan is someone who knows how to build and to plant. I know this firsthand as I have had the privilege for the last five years of leading the church that he planted – Hope Church, Craigavon. I have built upon strong and solid foundations that were laid by Alan and his wife Jan, and by God's grace, this congregation is flourishing.

Alan is also someone who knows how to uproot and tear down. When he moved from South Africa to Northern Ireland, he arrived into a setting deeply bound by religious tradition and a sectarian/political spirit. Alan immediately recognised that this was not how God wanted things to be. Some pastors would have left it alone. Others would have quietly moved on. Not Alan. With great courage, conviction, and compassion he tore down false altars and confronted cultural idols.

I don't know many who would have had the boldness and faith to press through the relentless opposition that Alan faced. Yet, he kept going until many of that congregation found abundant life and true freedom in Christ.

Where did Alan find the strength? How was he sustained during this deeply intense season?

It was through hearing the voice of God.

Each day Alan immersed himself in the Word of God and waited for the Spirit of God to speak to him.

That was his nourishment. That was his daily bread. That was his sustenance in the wilderness. That was how he found direction for the difficult decisions he had to make.

We are living in days of great turmoil and turbulence, confusion and chaos. More than ever, each one of us must hear the voice of God. We need direction and discernment. We need clarity and courage. We need wisdom and revelation.

In this book you will find all of the above. Alan has set aside considerable time to listen to what the Holy Spirit is saying to His children in this hour. We have the blessing and benefit of listening into the conversation.

I have no doubt that as you read 'Jesus Says' and reflect on these words, you will be encouraged and inspired. But even more than that, you will be nourished with bread from heaven.

"Whoever has ears, let them hear what the Spirit says to the churches." (Revelation 3:22)

Rev. Craig Cooney, Lead Pastor, HOPE Church, Craigavon and author of 'The Tension of Transition', Instagram: @daily.prophetic

INTRODUCTION

When God speaks things change. They have to. They can't stay the same. If you don't believe me then read the story of Lazarus. Dead and buried and all wrapped up, he could not resist the voice of Jesus speaking his name to come back to life.

There are so many voices competing for our attention. May times we listen to them rather than listening to the voice we need to listen to.

These 'Jesus Says' writings are a collection of journal entries I made over a period of a few months as I sought to hear the voice of the Lord for my life. I offer them to you in the prayerful hope that you will be encouraged in your faith walk and that, like Lazarus, you would walk in the life of God in your life.

Our culture needs to hear the voice of Jesus. We need to speak prophetically as a prophetic family to our culture.

What we do today affects the future generations. It's not just about us. It's about our children, grandchildren and great grandchildren. What we choose to do now and who we will listen to will affect future generations. Our sons, daughters, grandsons, granddaughters and future generations will prophesy!

In each chapter I have left a space for you to journal, to listen to Jesus for yourself. Maybe you have never journaled before. That's okay. Ask Jesus to speak to you. Listen. Then write down what you hear. It may be a word, a sentence, a paragraph, a book! Hear what Jesus says to you and future generations because it's all about Jesus and His fame! You may notice that at the end of end 'The Heart of Jesus for You' sections I end the paragraph with three dots - that is simply my way of saying that Jesus is still speaking - there is always more to hear from Jesus. It always has been about Jesus, it is about Jesus and always will be about Jesus. I am so thankful for our partnership in the gospel.

1. VOICE

Scripture

The gatekeeper opens the gate for him, and the sheep listen to his voice. He calls his own sheep by name and leads them out. When he has brought out all his own, he goes on ahead of them, and his sheep follow him because they know his voice. But they will never follow a stranger; in fact, they will run away from him because they do not recognise a stranger's voice. (John 10:3-5)

I am the good shepherd; I know my sheep and my sheep know me— just as the Father knows me and I know the Father—and I lay down my life for the sheep. (John 10:14-15)

The Heart of Jesus for You

Jesus says: Listen to my voice and not the voices that are speaking from a worldly point of view. Listen to the wisdom of other disciples that have trusted me in faith for supernatural provision. Listen to my voice as my sheep know my voice and I will lead you beside still waters.

Some people will try to work things out with a worldly/ fleshly mindset. You may even try that and it may work for a season. Friends may even try to persuade you that you are being irresponsible and try to fix things for you or even try to fix you. In many situations you will have a cacophony of voices vying for your attention and giving you advice. Seek out my voice as my voice will speak the truth for you and the situation you are in. If you want fruit that will last then you need to listen to my voice and obey what I say. Walk by faith, not by sight. It is the more difficult thing to do, but it will bring me greater glory and others will be impacted by what they see…

Thought

I have discovered that the journey of faith can be challenging. Understatement. It has been a confusing at times for me. It has been even more confusing to some of my friends who are watching our faith story evolve. They cannot work out why we just do not do the normal thing. Surrender can look intimidating to others. It was intimidating to me and many times I have tried to work out a way forward, only to be reminded by the Lord to trust in Him and to wait. The voices of this world can be persuasive, but in the end they are not usually the voices of faith.

Jesus talks about the sheep following the voice of the shepherd, He speaks and they follow. A stranger speaks and they run away from the stranger's voice. Take time to listen for the voice of Jesus amongst all of the other competing voice's through Scripture, prayer and worship.

Jesus also said that the shepherd who speaks and calls his sheep is good. He does not abandon the sheep and he sacrifices himself for them. In your walk of faith know that in all the different seasons God is always good and that He has not abandoned you or forgotten you. The hired hand, those other voices and things of the world, will abandon you and let you down. Jesus will not.

As the Puritan William Gurnall[1] wrote: "We need to stand in the way God has directed us to walk. We are so prone to desire another's work than our own...The service you do out of your own path is not acceptable to the Lord.

---

[1] William Gurnall, The Christian in Complete Armour, 1:279-285

God will not thank you for doing that which He did not ask you to do."

Hear what the Lord is saying and walk in the path that he has directed you in.

What is Jesus saying to you?

2. LOVE

Scripture

There is no fear in love. But perfect love drives out fear, because fear has to do with punishment. The one who fears is not made perfect in love. (1 John 4:18)

The God of passionate love will meet with me. My God will empower me to rise in triumph over my foes. (Psalm 59:10, TPT)

The Heart of Jesus for You

Jesus says: My love for you is fierce. It is not a shallow, lukewarm love that is extinguished or diminished at the first sign of disobedience. It is a long lasting and constant love. My love for you cheers you on. I am your greatest cheerleader. My love for you disciplines you. My love for you works in and through you to bring a revelation of who I am to others. Lift up your head and do not let it drop! I love you and will not abandon you. But I do say this to you: train yourself in the power of the Holy Spirit to make wise choices and to grow in faith. I can redeem any choice that you make, but learn to grow in godly and pure choices that will bring me glory. Through that others will see how much I love you and them. I love you…

Thought

Love can be ferocious. Look at 1 John 4:18: "There is no fear in love. But perfect love drives out fear, because fear has to do with punishment. The one who fears is not made perfect in love." The words 'drive out' mean to throw or to cast. When God's love is allowed free rein in your life one of the first things to happen is for that love to go on a search and destroy mission on fear. As soon as it finds fear, God's love throws it out. Sometimes we may feel that the fear is still around. I believe that we feel that because, as God throws out the fear, we reach out a hand to hold onto it. For some strange reason we feel that we need or deserve the fear. The other issue for not letting go of fear is that we will have to surrender to the Lord absolutely everything. We may like the idea of surrender, but the actual practice of it can be rather more difficult. If we make choices out of fear then we make choices that we can control. If we surrender everything to God then we let Him take control and that can be frightening to us.

But note what the rest of the verse says: fear has to do with punishment. Why should you desire to be punished when there is no condemnation in Jesus? So, I invite you today to surrender to the fierce love of God and let Him drive out, cast out, throw out the fear in your life.

What is Jesus saying to you?

3. WAX

Scripture

May you blow them away like smoke—as wax melts before the fire, may the wicked perish before God. But may the righteous be glad and rejoice before God; may they be happy and joyful. (Psalm 68:2-3)

The mountains melt like wax before the LORD, before the Lord of all the Earth. (Psalm 97:5)

The Heart of Jesus for You

Jesus says: Hold on. You are not alone. It may feel like you are alone, but I am right there with you. Sometimes, when you focus on the fear, you turn your eyes away from me and forget I am right there beside you. But no matter what you feel the truth is, I am with you even if you are not looking at me or acknowledging me. I will never leave you or abandon you. You may say to me that you have done terrible things or that you have sinned too much. I say to you: I always forgive those who repent, no matter how many times you have to repent. Receive my love and forgiveness. Picture this: when you sin, think of sin as candle wax. The further you move away from the fire, the harder the wax becomes. The closer to the fire, then the wax melts. The further you go away from me the harder your heart will become. Draw near to the fire of my presence and let me soften your heart...

Thought

Thank goodness that "The reason the Son of God appeared to us was to destroy the Devil's work." (1 John 3:8b) It can often feel that the Devil's work is prospering in your life. You made a decision to walk in purity only to fall down yet again. You then see these acts turn into a cycle that only spirals downwards, even though your heart doesn't want to go that route. Hopelessness then sets in and the one who was once strong in the faith, you, has been hardened by ongoing sin.

The good news is that "No pit is so deep that God's love is not deeper still" (Corrie ten Boom). The picture of sin, like a piece of wax that hardens when it is taken from the heat, is very powerful to me. I saw many people covered in wax-like sin. They were unable to move or receive love due to the accumulation of wax on them. They were once so on fire and close to the Lord, but now they look like ancient statues as the wax-sin had hardened. Then the grace of the Lord crashed in with the fire of His presence and melted the wax-sin. You may feel that you are one of those wax statues. Hope is waiting for you. The Lord can hear the whisper of desire in your heart to be forgiven. He will draw near with the fire of His presence and the wax will melt and once again you will be free. Whisper your repentance to Him and experience His response.

What is Jesus saying to you?

4. POOR

Scripture

Blessed are the poor in spirit, for theirs is the kingdom of Heaven. (Matthew 5:3)

...let us draw near to God with a sincere heart and with the full assurance that faith brings, having our hearts sprinkled to cleanse us from a guilty conscience and having our bodies washed with pure water. (Hebrews 10:22)

The Heart of Jesus for You

Jesus says: Blessed are the poor in spirit for theirs is the kingdom of Heaven. Those who do not know their need of me will wander endlessly, going from nowhere to nowhere. Those who know how wretched they are will realise that the only way home is through me. Trying to work it out on your own will only take you away from me. Draw near to me and I will draw near to you. Being pure in spirit means realising that you just can't do it by yourself and that you need to depend upon me. Turn around and come back to me. Don't hesitate. I am waiting for you with open arms. Do not be scared, but come humbly and in repentance. My love covers all…

Thought

I suppose my life has been an ongoing discovery of how much I need the Lord. In my life I go through seasons of knowing that truth and then, for some reason or another, I forget, take hold of the steering wheel of my life and try to drive my life in a direction I think is right. Pride enters my heart and I walk away from the kingdom of Heaven. It constantly amazes me how forgiving and loving the Lord truly is.

The image of a loving father running to embrace and welcome his wayward child, in the story of the prodigal son, is all the more powerful as I recognise that I am that son and even though I have wandered aimlessly away, my Heavenly Father runs to me. He doesn't wait or ignore me or punish me, he runs to me and throws his arms around me and reminds me that I am his child.

We all absolutely need Jesus. Every single person on

planet Earth needs Jesus. He is the only way. He is the only truth and he is the only life.

Sometimes, the ways of the Lord can be painful. However, I must embrace them in order that I may know him and experience his life changing welcome.

What is Jesus saying to you?

5. DECLUTTER

Scripture

You are the light of the world. A town built on a hill cannot be hidden. (Matthew 5:14)

In the same way, let your light shine before others, that they may see your good deeds and glorify your Father in Heaven. (Matthew 5:16)

The Heart of Jesus for You

Jesus says: Don't dim in your shining. You are the light of the world, so shine brightly. You shine because I am in you. You have no light of your own. It is all from me. So, if you are dimming it is because you have less of me in you. It doesn't mean that I am disappearing within you. It means that something is blocking the light from shining. Now is the time to remove the clutter in you that is blocking and dimming my light in you. The people of this world need you to shine. Don't feel guilty; feel excited. Repentance is a good thing and it excites me and gladdens my heart when one of my children repents and declutters.

So let your light shine so that others will glorify me…

Thought

If there is more of the world in you, then there will be less of Jesus in you. You need to declutter your spiritual life so that it brings joy to you and to others. I do not like clutter and it is so debilitating when you go into a room that is full of stuff. You feel you can't move or breathe. The same happens with your spiritual life. The world and its cares can clutter up your spirit. If that happens your spirit can shrink and your worldly desires increase. The Holy Spirit in your spirit is meant to lead your body and soul, and not be led by them. If your spiritual light is dimming maybe it's because the worldly clutter in your life is covering the light of Jesus, just like a blanket suffocates a fire.

Now the thing that should excite you is the same thing that excites the Lord: repentance. I know repentance has had a bad press, but it is a wonderful thing that excites the heart of God. Repentance is the way you declutter your spirit and let more of Jesus in. It is taking the blanket from the fire so that the fire of God within you can once more again roar with life, as the breath of God blows upon you. So, repent, declutter and shine once again.

What is Jesus saying to you?

6. ABIDE

Scripture

Very early in the morning, while it was still dark, Jesus got up, left the house and went off to a solitary place, where he prayed. (Mark 1:35)

But when you pray, go into your room, close the door and pray to your Father, who is unseen. Then your Father, who sees what is done in secret, will reward you. (Matthew 6:6)

Remain in me, as I also remain in you. No branch can bear fruit by itself; it must remain in the vine. Neither can you bear fruit unless you remain in me. (John 15:4)

The Heart of Jesus for You

Jesus says: Don't leave me on the outside. Don't neglect to meet with me or talk with me each day. Don't forget our daily appointment. I so look forward to talking with you each day. Just being with me will give you the hope and strength for the day ahead. I understand that it is not always easy to find that time, but it will be worth it. Am I your greatest desire or do you have a greater treasure than me? Let me breathe the Holy Spirit upon you as I did to my disciples so long ago in a locked room after my resurrection. Abide in me and I will abide in you. Stay connected to me...

Thought

All fruitfulness that matters in our lives comes from intimacy with Jesus. That daily encounter with Jesus is vital to spiritual health and well-being. I get excited by the thought of having a quiet time with Jesus and an extra strong coffee. The idea of not having a quiet time with Jesus never enters my head. That is not because I'm holy or special. It's just that my wife and I have cultivated the discipline of connecting with Jesus every single day. It wasn't always like that in my life. For years I struggled with having a quiet time and then something clicked. I can't tell you what it was. Maybe it was perseverance. All I know is that I have to start my day with Jesus. Three verses encourage me to do that:

- Trust in the LORD with all your heart and lean not

on your own understanding; in all your ways submit to him, and he will make your paths straight (Pro 3:5-6)

- Let the morning bring me word of your unfailing love, for I have put my trust in you. Show me the way I should go, for to you I entrust my life (Psalms 143:8)

- In the morning, LORD, you hear my voice; in the morning I lay my requests before you and wait expectantly (Psalm 5:3)

It is impossible for a follower of Jesus to survive and grow without connecting with Him each day. It is pretty clear that fruitfulness comes from intimacy with Jesus:

- I am the vine; you are the branches. If you remain in me and I in you, you will bear much fruit; apart from me you can do nothing (John 15:5)

One of the tools I have found to be so helpful is journaling. Sometimes, I don't write much. Sometimes, I write a lot. I love to process my thoughts and emotions on paper. I write prayers. I listen to what I feel the Lord is saying to me and write those thoughts down - which is where 'Jesus says' came from. It is never too late. Get into His presence today and start a daily time with Jesus and listen to what Jesus is saying to you.

What is Jesus saying to you?

7. FARAWAY

Scripture

When he came to his senses, he said, "How many of my father's hired servants have food to spare, and here I am starving to death!" (Luke 15:17)

Brothers and sisters, if someone is caught in a sin, you who live by the Spirit should restore that person gently. But watch yourselves, or you also may be tempted. (Galatians 6:1)

The Heart of Jesus for You

Jesus says: Speak gently and tenderly to those who walk away from me. Do not judge them, but continue to love them and to connect with them. They have not reached the end of their story with me. Even if they go far away from me, let them come back to their senses and let them come back to me when it is time. I am still with them even if they do not acknowledge me at the moment. I love them so much and my heart breaks for them. Have hope for those who seem to be too far gone and have made apparently irreversible decisions. I can once again transform them and restore them and renew them. Have hope and let them know that they are loved. Do not abandon them. Abandonment is like a hammer that drives the nail of untruth deeper into the heart. Have my hope for them…

Thought

Critical judgement has no place in the life of a disciple of Jesus. Jesus taught us: "Do not judge and you will not be judged. Do not condemn and you will not be condemned. Forgive and you will be forgiven." (Luke 6:37). The standard of Jesus in relationships is higher than the standard of the world. Do not just love others who love you, but love your enemies. Love those who revile you. Love those who make fun of you. Love those who work against you. Love those who are living sinful lives. Love those who used to worship me but no longer do. Love, love, love. Love those people who were once followers of Jesus, but no longer are. We make people prayer points, but really all we are doing a lot of the time, is gossiping.

Jesus says: Do not judge people. Stop it.

It is also easy to lose hope for those that we love and are far away from Jesus. Some of you have family members who have made decisions and seems impossible for them to come back to Jesus. God has not abandoned them. God invades impossible lives and situations and brings transformation, repentance, forgiveness and hope. They are not too far gone. Stop telling them what they shouldn't be doing or reminding them of all the mistakes that they may have made, and pray for them all the more and love them with generous love.

What is Jesus saying to you?

8. PLAN A

Scripture

"Lord, if it's you," Peter replied, "tell me to come to you on the water." "Come," he said. Then Peter got down out of the boat, walked on the water and came toward Jesus. (Matthew 14:28-29)

And my God will meet all your needs according to the riches of his glory in Christ Jesus. (Philippians 4:19)

The Heart of Jesus for You

Jesus says: Walk on water with me. Step out of the boat and do something that takes faith in me. No Plan B, only plan A – which is me. I am your plan A. When you step out of the boat, it may seem that the waves are bigger than you thought and that the situation is more impossible. But, it is the same situation that you stepped into by faith. The waves are the same size as when you were back in the boat, and I am not taken by surprise. It is just that you have abandoned all your worldly and external props and you stand with naked faith in the face of a chaotic storm

and your only hope is me. Do not be afraid. I will never let you down and the adventure will only get greater and your faith will only get stronger...
Thought

I suppose it is human instinct to look for multiple options for a given situation. I love keeping my options open! It brings a feeling of safety and security and the sense that if one thing fails then we have another option to go with. As a disciple of Jesus there is no such way forward. There are no multiple options from which we can choose. There is only one option and that option is Jesus. There's only one plan and that plan is Jesus. There is no Plan B. If you think about it, you can see why. If we had a Plan A (Jesus) and then a Plan B (my option) then what we are saying is that there's always the possibility that Jesus will fail. If He does, then we will do it our own way. Do you see how crazy that thought process is? It betrays a lack of faith in Jesus. It creates unbelief.

This story of George Mueller is inspirational:[2] *"The*

_____

[2] https://www.christianity.com/church/church-history/church-history-for-kids/george-mueller-orphanages-built-by-prayer-11634869.html

children are dressed and ready for school. But there is no food for them to eat," the housemother of the orphanage informed George Mueller. George asked her to take the 300 children into the dining room and have them sit at the tables. He thanked God for the food and waited. George knew God would provide food for the children as he always did. Within minutes, a baker knocked on the door. "Mr. Mueller," he said, "last night I could not sleep. Somehow, I knew that you would need bread this morning. I got up and baked three batches for you. I will bring it in."

Soon, there was another knock at the door. It was the milkman. His cart had broken down in front of the orphanage. The milk would spoil by the time the wheel was fixed. He asked George if he could use some free milk. George smiled as the milkman brought in ten large cans of milk. It was just enough for the 300 thirsty children.

Jesus said: I am the way, the truth and the life. Full stop. There is no other way to the Father apart from Jesus. No other truth, but Jesus. No other life, but Jesus. No other place, but Jesus. The church and the world needs men and women of faith to rise up and live a life of complete surrender. No other plan, but Jesus.

What is Jesus saying to you?

9. TIME

Scripture

When he opened the seventh seal, there was silence in Heaven for about half an hour. (Revelation 8:1)

A thousand years in your sight are like a day that has just gone by, or like a watch in the night. (Psalms 90:4)

The Heart of Jesus for You

Jesus says: Time is not an issue for me. It doesn't matter if the situation is one day old or 30 years old. I am time-full. I can transform and heal any breakthrough no matter how long the impossible situation has been in place. I can time travel. The woman with the issue of blood continued to have faith, despite having nothing and she was healed after being ill for 12 years. The man by the pool of Siloam was healed despite being disabled for 30 years with no one to help him. In the difficult and impossible situations let me shape you and form you and let me grow your faith. Even dreams that have been dead and buried and wrapped up in grave clothes can once again come back to life. Remember Lazarus. Even though Lazarus had been dead for three days, it was not too late for me to bring life to him. You are not too far from hope. There is not a line you can cross and then all hope is gone…

Thought

Sometimes, when trusting in the Lord, it can seem as though he has let us down. We may have been waiting for something to happen and the deadline has passed. Nothing has happened. It can sometimes feel like the Lord is just too late and it can be frustrating if someone says that God's timing is perfect.

Mary and Martha, sisters of Lazarus, learnt all of this through difficult experience. In their eyes it was necessary for Jesus to come and heal their brother before he died. To them, no miracles could happen after death. Jesus waited deliberately until Lazarus had died and then arrived. His explanation to the disciples was incredible: "Lazarus is dead and for your sake I am glad I was not there so that you may believe." (John 11:14-15) Jesus said to Martha: "I am the resurrection and the life." (John 11:25)

I know that this may be a difficult truth for some to accept at the moment, but it is not all about us. The universe is not human-centric, it is God-centric. It's all about Him and His glory. God wants us to know Him and for Him to get all the glory. Who else would get the glory? Us? That's idolatry. He is the only one worthy of all glory. Jesus said: "I'm glad I was not there so that you may believe." It's all about the Lord, but he made a delay so other people will believe in him. God is bigger than us. Could it be that God is not time-less, but time-full and that means that the delays are all for His glory and to bring others to the place of belief? Do not despair in the midst of a delay.

What is Jesus saying to you?

10. WORRY

Scripture

Therefore I tell you, do not worry about your life, what you will eat or drink; or about your body, what you will wear. Is not life more than food, and the body more than clothes? (Matthew 6:25)

Can any one of you by worrying add a single hour to your life? (Matthew 6:27)

And why do you worry about clothes? See how the flowers of the field grow. They do not labour or spin. (Matthew 6:28)

So do not worry, saying, "What shall we eat?" or "What shall we drink?" or "What shall we wear?" (Matthew 6:31)

But seek first His kingdom and His righteousness, and all these things will be given to you as well. (Matthew 6:33)

Therefore do not worry about tomorrow, for tomorrow will worry about itself. Each day has enough trouble of its own. (Matthew 6:34)

The Heart of Jesus for You

Jesus says: Do not worry. Do not be anxious. It is a waste of time to expend energy worrying about things that you cannot change. Instead, learn to trust me more in the situations you're worrying about. Hand them over to me in prayer. I understand it is easy to talk about doing that, but more difficult to actually do it. But, it is still the truth. If you want peace, then pray to me about every situation. How do you do that? First, worship. Second, pray. Third, surrender all. It is learning to be a living sacrifice and letting me control the situation. That is true freedom. That is true faith. Continue to follow me on the narrow road. Do not get disheartened as I am still with you and I have not abandoned the situation you're concerned about. Remember I am the way, the truth and the life of absolutely everything…

Thought

I suspect that 'Do not worry' is probably one of the most difficult commands of Jesus to follow. It just seems to come so naturally to many of us. Sometimes, it can seem uncaring not to worry! Someone may say, 'If I don't worry about them, then it shows that I don't really care about them.' That is a lie. We are expressly told by Jesus not to worry about anything and to live one day at a time, yet we disregard this command of Jesus and worry. A lot.

Jesus tells us not to worry about what we will eat, what we will drink, what clothes we are to have. Jesus says: "Can any one of you by worrying add a single hour to your life?" (Matthew 6:27) Jesus goes further and basically says this: "If you are worried about these things then you're living a pagan lifestyle. You are living without reference to God and that is atheism."

Oswald Chambers wrote: "The secret of Christian quietness is not indifference, but the knowledge that God is my Father, He loves me, I shall never think of anything He will forget and worry becomes an impossibility." Oswald Chambers has got it so right. It's not about being indifferent about the things that concern us, but about handing them over to the care of God and then trusting him with the situation. Then we can stand back in peace.

Worry also makes our concerns and cares the centre of attention. If we worry, we are saying, "We are the most important, so give me what I want and give me the outcome I desire." Jesus responds by saying: "Seek first His kingdom and His righteousness and all these things will be given to you as well." (Matthew 6:33)

What is Jesus saying to you?

11. OTHERS

Scripture

He answered, "'Love the Lord your God with all your heart and with all your soul and with all your strength and with all your mind'; and, 'Love your neighbour as yourself.'" (Luke 10:27)

Two are better than one. (Ecclesiastes 4:9)

Plans fail for lack of counsel, but with many advisers they succeed. (Proverbs 15:22)

The Heart of Jesus for You

Jesus says: You need other people. You may think that you do not need anyone else, but you were made to be in relationship - even introverts. It is the only way that you will make progress. You need others. That is why I gathered twelve disparate disciples. They didn't get on all of the time. They argued and didn't understand what was happening. However, they needed each other. Iron sharpens iron. Don't fall into the belief stronghold that you can do it all by yourself. If you think that, you will end up not needing my help, for I help you through others. Love those around you even though you may find some of them frustrating. You can sometimes be frustrating. Pray for each of them by name. Each one is precious in my sight and they each have their own story to tell. If you love one another the world will know that you are my disciples...

Thought

As an introvert I must confess that I can find people tiring and I often think that I can do something better than anyone else. Occasionally I can do it better, but more often they can do it just as well or much better than me. One of the lessons it has taken me the longest to learn is that I need other people and they need me. The church is a congregation, a gathering of people, not a gathering of bricks.

We need other people who rub us up the wrong way, people who disagree with us, who say the wrong thing, those who like hymns on an organ, whilst you like contemporary worship music. We all need each other.

Here are three reasons why:

(1) God is in community. He is perfect community. This is a basic trinitarian concept that God is in community - Father, Son and Holy Spirit. Community is modelled in the Trinity and that community is relational. God is not alone within Himself.

(2) Iron sharpens iron (Proverbs 27:17). Other people and all of their foibles make us better people and more like Jesus, if we are in relationship with them.

(3) There are so many 'one another's' in the New Testament: Be devoted to one another, honour one another above yourselves, live in harmony with one another (Romans 12:10,16). Love one another (Romans 13:8). Stop passing judgement on one another (Romans 14:13). Accept one another (Romans 15:7). Greet one another with a holy kiss (Romans 16:16). And all of these are the ones in Romans, a deeply theological book. I understand that it is difficult to get on with everyone. Some might even be considered an enemy. In every case, LOVE THEM.

As a friend in Iris Ministries said, "Even solitary lions can be taken out."

What is Jesus saying to you?

12. REFRESHED

Scripture

Nehemiah said, "Go and enjoy choice food and sweet drinks, and send some to those who have nothing prepared. This day is holy to our Lord. Do not grieve, for the joy of the LORD is your strength." (Nehemiah 8:10)

The LORD your God is with you, the Mighty Warrior who saves. He will take great delight in you; in his love he will no longer rebuke you, but will rejoice over you with singing. (Zephaniah 3:17-18)

The Heart of Jesus for You

Jesus says: Today I will refresh you and you will not be tired, weary or down hearted, but I will refresh you, strengthen you and bring joy into your heart. Some of you have not known joy for a while. That is going to change. I say it again: that is going to change. I am the Joy Bringer and I am imparting my joy to you. When I impart my joy you will be strengthened and refreshed. You don't become strong to be joyful. You become joyful to be strong.

Weariness often comes when you're trying too hard to do things or work things out in your own strength. This is all too big for you to work out and make happen, so lean on me. Take up my yoke. Cling to me rather than cling to the problems or situations. Trust me because I know what I'm doing...

Thought

The journey of faith is tiring. The daily surrender and the unknown can be exhausting. Not knowing what is going to happen next can drain us of energy. Surrender is hard work. The first stage excitement of surrender is 'exhilaration' and we cry "yes" to the Lord at a conference or a gathering where we have been inspired and challenged. I found the second stage of surrender is 'struggle'. It is where the rubber hits the road.

We simply want to do what the Lord wants, but when nothing seems to be happening or no door seems to open, we take the steering wheel of our life back from the Lord. We know we shouldn't, but we want something to happen. We give control back and then we take it away again and we enter a cycle of surrender and survival. The third stage of surrender is 'peace'. You get to the stage when you can truly hand over everything to the Lord and you just don't worry about tomorrow and you are thankful for today.

Psalm 23:3 tells us that God refreshes our soul. The word 'refreshes' can also mean 'restores'. We can try things to encourage our soul and that is not a bad thing. Ultimately, however, refreshment and restoration come from the Lord. Get back into His presence. Receive from Him. Hand back control to Him. Don't hold onto the problems, but cling to Jesus instead.

What is Jesus saying to you?

13. DANCE

Scripture

…a time to weep and a time to laugh, a time to mourn and a time to dance (Ecclesiastes 3:4)

Now the Lord is the Spirit, and where the Spirit of the Lord is, there is freedom. (2 Corinthians 3:17)

The Heart of Jesus for You

Jesus says: Dance with me. I know that you think you're not a dancer, but when you let me lead in the dance you are amazing. It's when you try to lead that you stumble. Trust me to lead you and you will find freedom, exhilaration and a life free from worry. It is in the spinning and the twirls of the dance that you will find an exciting weightlessness that will lift you up rather than wear you down.

Dance with me and let me lead, for in doing that I will teach you new steps and new moves. You will discover that you can do things that you didn't realise you could do. You will find that you can dance on water, even in a storm.

You will find that you can dance in captivity and in time of lack. You will find that you can dance in times of fear. You will be able to dance and worship your way through the storm. Come with me and let us dance together…

Thought

I am not a dancer. I do appreciate the waltz and, for some reason, tap dancing - although I can do neither. The idea of dancing does not fill me with joy! I suppose it's the thought that I might look silly and self-conscious. I can remember one morning in Northern Ireland, where the Lord challenged me to dance in the kitchen. I was not feeling spiritual or close to the Lord, but I clearly heard him telling me to stand up and dance around the kitchen as an act of obedience to him and to dance on the negative things that I had been feeling. I even wrote a little song that I sang as I danced around the kitchen. Another time, Jan and I danced around the nave of the church. It was where I preached from. On either side were seats where the choir would sit. Many of whom did not like the freedom of the Holy Spirit. I felt spiritual oppression when I preached.

Jan and I decided to dance around the area when no one was there. After that, many things changed in a dramatic way. Dancing with Jesus seems so poetic and ethereal, but He is calling you into a freedom dance. Maybe it is actually dancing. Maybe it is doing something that you know you need to do, but it makes you feel uncomfortable. Let Jesus lead and move you into a new freedom.

What is Jesus saying to you?

14. FAMILY

Scripture

Now when David had served God's purpose in his own generation, he fell asleep; he was buried with his ancestors and his body decayed. (Acts 13:36)

Then we your people, the sheep of your pasture, will praise you forever; from generation to generation we will proclaim your praise. (Psalms 79:13)

The Heart of Jesus for You

Jesus says: Trust me with your family. Trust your children to me. I have a better plan for them than you do. I love them more than you do. Trust me with your children, your grandchildren and your great-grandchildren. I am not just a one-generation Saviour. I save multiple generations. Trust me with your parents, your brothers and your sisters. Trust me with those you haven't spoken to for such a long time, but you still love. I am the Lord. I am the way, the truth and the life. There is no other. I created family. I planted a family in the garden of Eden. I restore family.

Hand them over to me. Hand me your wayward children and your family members. Don't lose hope. Have faith that they will come back to their senses. Let me take your anxiety about your family members and in place of the anxiety take my peace...

Thought

I have four adult children, two grandchildren and one son-in-law. I love them all dearly and truly want God's best for them. I know that we shouldn't worry, but my greatest worry/struggle is my family. I want to protect and provide for them. I want to fix things for them. I want to try and work things out for them. This has been more difficult for me over the past four years, as we have lived by faith with no fixed abode. So this is something I really have had to work at and daily have to hand over to the Lord.

In Mary's Song in Luke 1:50, there is a lovely phrase that so encourages me. It says: "His mercy extends to those who fear him from generation to generation." The mercy of the Lord extends to my children and grandchildren and great-grandchildren. He has a better plan for your children than you do. He has his hand upon your grandchildren. Each day I pray for my children and grandchildren and great-grandchildren even though I do not have any great-grandchildren yet. Pray for the generations not yet born. If you do not have children, pray for your nieces and nephews, your friends' children or children in your church. Lift them up to the Lord and let us see him work out the purpose of God in their generation (Acts 13:36).

What is Jesus saying to you?

15. PROCESS

Scripture

Commit to the Lord whatever you do, and he will establish your plans. (Proverbs 16:3)

Many are the plans in a person's heart, but it is the Lord's purpose that prevails. (Proverbs 19:21)

To humans belong the plans of the heart, but from the Lord comes the proper answer of the tongue. (Proverbs 16:1)

The Heart of Jesus for You

Jesus says: Trust and surrender to the process. I invite you to submit to the process I'm taking you through. You may not understand why things are happening to you the way they are. You may even feel abandoned or demoted to the back of the line. You may feel forgotten or that things are just too difficult. But, I invite you to submit to the process and trust the process I have set in motion.

I know that you have a plan all worked out in your head of what you think should happen, and I realise you think it is a better plan, but my way will bear more fruit in you and in others. Your faith will grow. The warrior in you will become stronger. Comfort and ease do not make spiritual warriors. Faith is not grown by having everything go the way that you want it to go.

I am preparing you for eternity, not just for the rest of your life on Earth. There is an eternal glory waiting for you and the preparation for that starts now. I even use affliction to shape you and purify you. Do not be surprised. Keep going. Do not give up. Trust my process…

Thought

God has a plan and a process. Psalm 33:11 says: "…but the plans of the Lord stand firm forever, the purpose of his heart through all generations."Most of the time I don't understand the plans and process of the Lord or I can't see or sense what He is doing. It does frustrate me at times and I have to hand that frustration to Him and take another step of faith in Him. I declare my faith in Him. I worship Him.

Sometimes, Scripture can be brutal. It says in Proverbs

24:10: "…if you falter in times of trouble, how small is your strength." Maybe that is what is happening in this process you are going through. God uses tough situations to make you stronger, so that you can go and not falter in the next stage of the journey of faith. Maybe we have become too soft in our Christian faith and the Lord is toughening us up. The disciples didn't always understand the process and plans of Jesus. After saying that the son of man would be killed it says, "…the disciples didn't understand any of this…" (Luke 18:32). I know how they feel. It's okay not to understand anything or to feel frustrated. Just keep following Jesus one step at a time.

What is Jesus saying to you?

16. NAME

Scripture

Whoever acknowledges me before others, I will also acknowledge before my Father in Heaven. But whoever disowns me before others, I will disown before my Father in Heaven. (Matthew 10:32-33)

Therefore God exalted him to the highest place and gave him the name that is above every name, that at the name of Jesus every knee should bow, in Heaven and on Earth and under the Earth, and every tongue acknowledge that Jesus Christ is Lord, to the glory of God the Father. (Philippians 2:9-11)

But these are written that you may believe that Jesus is the Messiah, the Son of God, and that by believing you may have life in his name. (John 20:31)

And whatever you do, whether in word or deed, do it all in the name of the Lord Jesus, giving thanks to God the Father through him. (Colossians 3:17)

The Heart of Jesus for You

Jesus says: Do not be afraid to actually speak my name in the presence of those who don't yet follow me. Many use my name in anger and frustration. You can speak my name in love and power. As you speak my name, people may be offended as you say it in love and adoration and it may be a stumbling block to some. However, as they stumble I plan to pick them up and invite them to follow me. There is power in my name and people need to hear my name. So, do not be afraid of speaking my name. As you say my name it will be like the affect of the oil when I was anointed by the surrendered woman in the house where I was eating. The fragrance and effect of her act filled the house and, as you speak and declare my name, the fragrance of that surrendered act will leave a fragrance and effect that will linger and be absorbed by people. You will meet some of them in glory…

Thought

Sometimes, I feel that the only time you hear the name of Jesus, outside the context of church, is when His name taken in vain. I sometimes feel that Christians are nervous about using the name of Jesus, not in vain, but in conversation with people. Why are we so embarrassed to say that we are disciples of Jesus? What are you going to lose by saying that you follow Jesus? Some people may think you are crazy and some people may be intrigued.

I feel that when we say the name of Jesus in conversation it is like the women who anointed the feet of Jesus in John Chapter 12. She goes into a hostile environment for her, focuses on Jesus, pours everything she has on Him and wipes His feet with her hair. Lazarus, whom Jesus had raised from the dead, was there. The disciples were there. A large crowd was there, eager to see Jesus and the man Lazarus. Into the mix add the fact that the chief priests were planning to kill Lazarus! It was a chaotic and crazy situation and into it walked Mary and simply adored Jesus. Verse 3 says: and the house was filled with the fragrance of the perfume. Mary's act touched everyone present. Speaking the name of Jesus is not a neutral act. It has power and it changes the surroundings and affects people. Speak his name out loud now: JESUS.

What is Jesus saying to you?

17. FEAR

Scripture

So, do not fear, for I am with you; do not be dismayed, for I am your God. I will strengthen you and help you; I will uphold you with my righteous right hand. (Isaiah 41:10)

There is no fear in love. But perfect love drives out fear, because fear has to do with punishment. The one who fears is not made perfect in love. (1 John 4:18)

The LORD is with me; I will not be afraid. What can mere mortals do to me? (Psalms 118:6)

The Heart of Jesus for You

Jesus says: Do not fear. Have a taster day today of choosing not to worry about anything. Give it a try and trust me. Cast all your cares on me and each time where your fear starts to rise, call on my name and throw all of your cares and fears on to me. What is the use of holding onto them if you can do nothing about them? They can cause you to have physical and mental ill-health. Do you think that by holding onto your fears they will change or get better? Do you think I could do something about your fears? Open your hands and release what you're holding onto. Your fears and worries are not a comfort blanket. If you want to walk into all I have planned for you, you need to let go of the fears and worries that grip you. Trust me and do not lean on your own understanding. If you don't, then fear will overwhelm you. Let me in and let me help you. You can either be overwhelmed by the situation or you can be overwhelmed by me. What do you want?...

Thought

Fear grows when you move away from Jesus. The further you go away from Him, the greater the potential for fear. Fear grows when your faith is low. In Luke 8:22-29 we read the story of the disciples of Jesus in a storm. He reprimanded them for lack of faith: "Where is your faith?" he asked his disciples. In fear and amazement they asked one another, "Who is this? He commands even the winds and the water, and they obey him." (Luke 8:25)

As far as I can see only one thing that amazed Jesus was

a lack of faith and there is only one way to please God and that is by faith.

The story of Jesus and the storm tells us three things:

1. Storms will happen in life. Most of the time the storms are not from God and we are called to stand firm by faith. In these times we stand by faith on the promises of God: "being confident of this, that he who began a good work in you will carry it on to completion until the day of Christ Jesus." (Philippians 1:6), "So do not fear, for I am with you; do not be dismayed, for I am your God. I will strengthen you and help you; I will uphold you with my righteous right hand." (Isaiah 41:10)

2. Jesus is with you all of the time in the storm. The disciples were not alone in the boat. Jesus was sleeping and by what they said, it sounded that the disciples were offended by that: "Teacher, don't you care if we drown?" (Mark 4:38). How many times have you said that in difficult situations? Don't you care God? Wake up God! Where are you God? However, He is always right there with you.

3. Jesus has the power, authority and desire to calm the

storms in your life. So, call upon Him to do just that and, with patient faith, watch what He does.

What is Jesus saying to you?

18. BREAKTHROUGH

Scripture

I have given you authority to trample on snakes and scorpions and to overcome all the power of the enemy; nothing will harm you. (Luke 10:19)

The light shines in the darkness, and the darkness has not overcome it. (John 1:5)

Do not grieve, for the joy of the LORD is your strength. (Nehemiah 8:10)

The Heart of Jesus for You

Jesus says: My child, I am here. Breakthrough is here. The next step is here. The time of silence is over. The time for affliction is ending. It is time for you to move onto the next lesson and the next lesson is a lesson in joy. It will be a time of learning how to be joyful in easy times and hard times. It will not be a forced or false joy. What I have been doing with you in this season that is now ending has brought a depth of strength that you have not had before. Stand strong. Stand up. Look into my eyes and rejoice in each situation. Look at my servants Paul and Silas who sang hymns in the dark prison. That's what you will be able to do. Pick up joy as a holy weapon to cut down all things that would come against you and pull you into their faithless claws. Your joy is a light that blinds the enemy. Your joy is from me and it is your strength. I sing over you with joy. Join me in the song...

Thought

It can seem that sometimes the next step is never going to come. That the promised breakthrough doesn't materialise - at least in the time frame that we would like. Each stage that we find ourselves in is an opportunity to learn something that will strengthen us, encourage us and bring glory to the Lord. Meditate on these breakthrough verses and worship the Lord:

2 Corinthians 9:8 - "And God is able to bless you abundantly, so that in all things at all times, having all that you need, you will abound in every good work."

2 Samuel 5:20 - "So David went to Baal Perazim, and there he defeated them. He said, "As waters break out, the

LORD has broken out against my enemies before me." So that place was called Baal Perazim."

Acts 1:8 - "But you will receive power when the Holy Spirit comes on you; and you will be my witnesses in Jerusalem, and in all Judea and Samaria, and to the ends of the Earth."

Deuteronomy 8:18 - "But remember the LORD your God, for it is he who gives you the ability to produce wealth, and so confirms his covenant, which he swore to your ancestors, as it is today."

Ephesians 3:20 - "Now to him who is able to do immeasurably more than all we ask or imagine, according to his power that is at work within us..."

Ephesians 6:18 - "And pray in the Spirit on all occasions with all kinds of prayers and requests. With this in mind, be alert and always keep on praying for all the Lord's people."

Hebrews 4:12 - "For the word of God is alive and active. Sharper than any double-edged sword, it penetrates even to dividing soul and spirit, joints and marrow; it judges the thoughts and attitudes of the heart."

Micah 2:13 - "The One who breaks open the way will go up before them; they will break through the gate and go out. Their King will pass through before them, the LORD at their head."

What is Jesus saying to you?

19. STAY

Scripture

From this time many of his disciples turned back and no longer followed him. "You do not want to leave too, do you?" Jesus asked the Twelve. Simon Peter answered him, "Lord, to whom shall we go? You have the words of eternal life. We have come to believe and to know that you are the Holy One of God." (John 6:66-68)

My soul faints with longing for your salvation, but I have put my hope in your word. (Psalms 119:81)

If your law had not been my delight, I would have perished in my affliction. (Psalms 119:92)

The Heart of Jesus for You

Jesus says: Don't turn away from me now. Where would you go? I know there have been difficulties and that you are at the end of your tether, that you feel as though you cannot continue, but if you leave me, where else would you go? I have the words of eternal life. Let me speak those words into your heart. I am the holy one of

God and, deep within, you know that I am the only way through this. Delight yourself in me. You can try and comfort yourself with other things, but ultimately I am your greatest treasure and I forgive you for wandering off the narrow path. Now is the time to get back onto the path. Stop inhabiting the castle of doubt and use the key of faith and repentance to be free once again. Don't turn away from me because I have never turned away from you and I never will...

Thought

On my journey of faith there have been so many times that I have wanted to give up or simply make something happen. There have been brief moments when I wondered whether I made the right decision surrendering all. That may sound shocking, but I need to be honest. The journey of faith can be difficult.

In John chapter 6 Jesus teaches about the bread of life. He chastises the people for following Him because they only did so because they saw the miracle of the multiplication of bread and fish. Jesus says to them: "Do not work for food that spoils, but for food that endures to eternal life, which the Son of Man will give you." (John 6:27) Jesus, a few verses later, declares: "I am the bread of life." (John 6:35) He later ends His teaching by saying that whoever eats His flesh and drinks His blood, He will remain in them and they in Him. (John 6:53-56) In the next passage the disciples are questioning Jesus. They found His teaching too hard. They say: "This is a hard teaching. who can accept it?" (John 6:60) The reading continues: "From this time many of his disciples turned back and no longer followed him." (John 6:68) Jesus then asked His disciples if they were going to leave too. Peter answered: "Lord to whom should we go? You have the words of eternal life."

In those times when I feel like it's all too hard and I want to give up, I think of those words that Peter said: "Jesus, where else would I go?"

What is Jesus saying to you?

20. DOORS

Scripture

Let the morning bring me word of your unfailing love, for I have put my trust in you. Show me the way I should go, for to you I entrust my life. (Psalms 143:8)

And pray for us, too, that God may open a door for our message, so that we may proclaim the mystery of Christ, for which I am in chains. (Colossians 4:3)

I know your deeds. See, I have placed before you an open door that no one can shut. I know that you have little strength, yet you have kept my word and have not denied my name. (Revelation 3:8)

The Heart of Jesus for You

Jesus says: In this next season, or as you try to discern what the next step is, don't try to force doors open. By all means try the handle and see if it turns, but don't try and force the door open. If you go through a door you have forced open you will end up doing that role or be in that season in your own strength. Not because I've abandoned you, but because you've turned your back on me and are going your own way. You are leaning on your own understanding. Sometimes, I may open two or three doors and invite you to choose to go through any of them. Sometimes, I will create a new doorway or create a new pathway where there's been none before. Don't let frustration dictate what you do. Frustration mutes faith, raises tension in your mind and body and it is a lousy guide. Hold my hand and walk with me in the way I will take you…

Thought

We were staying in a hotel as we transited through Johannesberg, O.R. Tambo Airport. As we went up to find our room we walked down one of the longest corridors I've been in. There were doors on either side as far as I could see. I felt that on our journey of faith it can sometimes be like getting stuck in a long corridor with locked doors on either side. There are so many opportunities behind each door, but each one is locked to me. In that corridor of life I have, in frustration, tried to open several doors, but the Lord didn't allow me to open them. In the corridor of life in which we found ourselves, I pushed at least 25 doors. Each door was closed and I must confess that I felt rejection after rejection difficult to take and my confidence in myself and my abilities was knocked. As I talked to Jan she said to me that maybe the Lord was teaching me to trust in His abilities and not in my abilities. That is truth. I amaze myself at how often I find myself forgetting it's not about my glory or renown. It's about the renown and glory of the Lord: "Yes Lord, walking in the ways of your laws, we wait for you; your name and your renown are the desires of our heart." (Isaiah 26:8) So, as I continue to try different doors I choose not to get frustrated, but choose to thank the Lord in every situation. I will not let the response I receive mute my faith, but I will let my faith grow and continue on the journey.

What is Jesus saying to you?

21. TIRED

Scripture

I will refresh the weary and satisfy the faint (Jeremiah 31:25)

...to whom he said, "This is the resting place, let the weary rest"; and, "This is the place of repose"— but they would not listen. (Isaiah 28:12)

He gives strength to the weary and increases the power of the weak. (Isaiah 40:29)

The Heart of Jesus for You

Jesus says: I know that you're tired and exhausted and you want to sleep a lot of the time. The pressures and stresses that you're under have caused a physical reaction in you and all you want to do is to sleep. If your body is telling you to rest, then rest and as you sleep I will visit you in your dreams. I will speak words of strength and comfort to you. But, in your tiredness do not let your guard down, spiritually or emotionally. As you sleep physically, do not go to sleep spiritually, I say it again: do not go to sleep spiritually. The Devil loves to keep Christians asleep and he loves to put temptation in front of them when they're tired and weak. As well as resting, I ask you to watch and pray. Stay alert to temptation. Worship. Read scripture. I will remind you of verses as you sleep. I will sing over you and my song will be like refreshing rain. You'll get through this and you'll be stronger as a result...

Thought

I wasn't busy during and after COVID. However, I did find myself getting tired physically and emotionally as we sought out what the Lord required of us and the direction in which He wanted us to go. It's okay to rest. It's good to sleep. But we must keep our spirits awake within us.

I recall waking up one morning and my spirit was singing before my body was awake. I know it sounds strange, but it was in the moments before my body woke up and my spirit was already singing praises to the Lord. My body roused itself and joined in the prayer and worship that was already going on.

We often use the phrase: body, soul and spirit. From

that we infer that the body is primary, with soul and the spirit having to follow the body. The Bible is different. It has the order: spirit, soul and body. It says 1 Thessalonians 5:23: "May your whole spirit soul and body be kept blameless at the coming of our Lord Jesus Christ." Our spirit leads our soul (emotions, thoughts and feelings) and our body. So, on the journey of faith ask the Lord to fill your spirit with the Holy Spirit. By all means rest and sleep physically, but let your spirit sing as you do.

What is Jesus saying to you?

22. IMPOSSIBLE

Scripture

Is anything too hard for the LORD? I will return to you at the appointed time next year, and Sarah will have a son. (Genesis 18:14)

Ah, Sovereign LORD, you have made the Heavens and the Earth by your great power and outstretched arm. Nothing is too hard for you. (Jeremiah 32:17)

For nothing will be impossible with God. (Luke 1:37, ESV)

Jesus looked at them and said, "With man this is impossible, but with God all things are possible.(Matthew 19:26)

The Heart of Jesus for You

Jesus says: Even though the situation you face looks impossible, it is impossible for me not to do the impossible. What looks like an insurmountable barrier to you, is to me a wall made of children's bricks that can be knocked down by a finger . When you need to cross a mighty ocean we can do one of two ways: Either you can try to walk across it alone or I can walk with you. Don't focus on the impossible, but focus on the God of the impossible. The weight of the impossible is too great a burden for you to carry. Let me carry it and don't focus on the worry part. When I called out the name of Lazarus, it was impossible for him to stay in the tomb. If I had not called him by name, everyone buried in the cemetery would have been raised from the dead. As I spoke to the blind eyes to be opened, it was impossible for them not to see. As I spoke to deaf ears, it was impossible for them not to hear. As I lay in the tomb after the crucifixion, it was impossible for me to stay dead. I am the God of life and it is impossible for me not to do the impossible...

Thought

Would we have built the ark in the middle of the desert believing that the Lord could cause it to rain? What would it have been like to have seen the Egyptian army charging at us from behind and a sea blocking our way ahead? How full of faith would we have been? When walking around the walls of Jericho would we have waited excitedly for the Lord to crash the walls down? Would our hearts be terrified, like the army of Israel, as they looked upon Goliath or would we have been like David, full of faith in the Lord and prepared to defy the giant before him? Would our courage have failed us as we walked to the lions' den? Would we be like Shadrach, Meshach and Abednego standing in front of the fiery furnace and declaring that if we are to be thrown into the blazing furnace then our God is able to save us from it, but even if he doesn't "we will not serve your gods?" (Daniel 3:17-18) We are part of the people of God, a people whose history is littered with men and women who trusted the Lord and let God do the impossible. He is the same God today and He is still doing the impossible through us and for us. Let faith arise!

What is Jesus saying to you?

23. WITNESS

Scripture

Now I want you to know, brothers and sisters, that what has happened to me has actually served to advance the gospel. As a result, it has become clear throughout the whole palace guard and to everyone else that I am in chains for Christ. And because of my chains, most of the brothers and sisters have become confident in the Lord and dare all the more to proclaim the gospel without fear. (Philippians 1:12-14)

The Heart of Jesus for You

Jesus says: Your faith and courage will be an inspiration for many other people. Don't give up and don't let your voice of faith be drowned out by your cries of fear. I want to hear you shout and see the walls crumble before you. Look at Jonathan and his shield-bearer. The two of them trusted me, went up against the Philistine army and moved forward in faith.[3] I came in power and the whole

---

[3] 1 Samuel 14

Israelite army was inspired by what they had done. Look
at David and Goliath. David trusted me, he won and he cut
off the enemy's head. The whole Israelite army, who stood
in fear, let out a battle cry and defeated the Philistines. Or
think of Paul in prison. His chains and the way he acted
led many people to follow me. Your faith and courage will
be an inspiration to many people...

Thought

As Paul was in prison he wrote these words: "Now, I
want you to know, brothers and sisters, that what has
happened to me has really served to advance the gospel."
(Phil 1:12) He goes on to give the proof of that statement.
First, people learnt more about Jesus. Secondly, followers
of Jesus were filled with courage by his example. (Phil 1:13)
How we act and live through difficult situations will be a
witness to other people. Some people just do not
understand our journey of faith. They want us to do the
sensible thing in their eyes. But we were not called to be
sensible. We were called to follow Jesus by faith and that
doesn't always look sensible. Our prayer is that our

discipleship will inspire others to greater faith.

The Greek word for 'witness' is 'martyr'. Martyr-ship involves cost. There is a cost to being a witness for Jesus. Your journey of faith is a witness to other people. People will be watching you. Don't let that be a pressure, but rather inspire you to keep on going and not to give up. Lives are being challenged, changed and encouraged by your journey of faith.

What is Jesus saying to you?

24. WAY

Scripture

For I know the plans I have for you," declares the LORD, "plans to prosper you and not to harm you, plans to give you hope and a future. (Jeremiah 29:11)

You provide a broad path for my feet, so that my ankles do not give way. (Psalms 18:36)

…he refreshes my soul. He guides me along the right paths for his name's sake. (Psalms 23:3)

The Heart of Jesus for You

Jesus says: I know that you can't see a way forward, but that doesn't mean that there isn't one. If you look with worldly eyes and you only see worldly truth, there is no way forward. To have hope and start to see a way forward you need to look at the circumstances with supernatural eyesight. You do that by not dwelling on the impossibilities. You do that by focusing on me and the dreams I have placed within you. Revisit the prophetic words spoken over you. Let faith arise and see the salvation of your Lord. When Abraham asked how he was going to have a child at his old age, he genuinely couldn't see a way forward. 'How can this be?' he asked. Yet he trusted me and I brought him an heir. The people of Israel could not see their way through the Red Sea and experienced real fear. Yet I provided a way through and they walked to safety. Mary asked the angel Gabriel: How can this be? The angel replied it can be because this is the will of God and it was so. I will make a way...

Thought

Jan and I were in Toronto for a short while at a time when we weren't sure what the next step was. We had finished leading churches, had given everything away and were basically living as nomads. Behind the house where we were staying was a pine forest and so we went for a walk. It was beautiful and sunny with the smell of pines filling the air. The tall straight trees were to be seen as far as the horizon. There was no path that we could see, so we wandered aimlessly between the trees. Until we suddenly stumbled on a long straight path. It was amazing. Walk a couple of steps backward and the path disappeared. Two steps forward and there again was a clear path. I knew that's exactly what it can feel like on the journey of faith. Some of you feel that you've been wandering aimlessly and, possibly you feel, hopelessly in a forest of fir trees where there is no path. Hold on and don't despair. "Stand at the crossroads and look; ask for the ancient paths, ask where the good way is, and walk in it, and you will find rest for your souls." (Heb 6:16)

What is Jesus saying to you?

25. FRUITFULNESS

Scripture

God blessed them and said, "Be fruitful and increase in number and fill the water in the seas, and let the birds increase on the Earth." (Genesis 1:22)

Then God blessed Noah and his sons, saying to them, Be fruitful and increase in number and fill the Earth. (Genesis 9:1)

The Heart of Jesus for You

Jesus says: I can bring fruitfulness into barren places. There is no such thing as hard ground to me. I can soften hearts and plant seeds that will bear much fruit. Abraham and Sarah were barren and I gave them a child. Isaac and Rebecca were barren and I gave them a child. Hannah and Elkanah were barren and I gave them a child. Elizabeth and Zachariah were barren and I gave them a child. However, I am not just talking about the physical fruit of children. I am also wanting to give you spiritual fruitfulness and abundance. Stay connected because fruit happens when you're connected to me. Barrenness and fruitfulness are both seasons in which I can teach you faith amongst many other things. Even though barrenness and the wilderness are difficult, I am there with you and in those places you will increasingly learn to rely on me. But, fruitfulness is coming...

Thought

One of my favourite verses in the Bible is: 'They spoke against God; they said can God really spread a table in the wilderness?' (Ps 78:19). The context of this verse is a history of the people of Israel, who were continuing to sin against the Lord despite his faithfulness. But, before we judge them, shouldn't we just pause and reflect whether we do the same thing? Of course we do. Verse 20 says: 'True, he struck the rock and water gushed out, streams flowed abundantly, but can you also give us bread? Can you supply meat for His people?' They acknowledged that God had done some good things, but in the same breath they questioned whether He could do more. Jesus says: 'If you remain in me and I in you, you will bear much fruit.' (John 15:5) There is no fruit for us apart from a connection to Jesus. You will be fruitful if you connect to Jesus. No question. If you aren't fruitful, then check your connection to Jesus. Is there sin in your life? Is your quiet time simply going through the motions? Is your spirit alive and full of the Holy Spirit? Even if you feel you are in a season of barrenness, remain close to Jesus because fruit will come! Stay connected to Jesus because then you will bear fruit.

What is Jesus saying to you?

26. FROGS

Scripture

If we confess our sins, he is faithful and just and will forgive us our sins and purify us from all unrighteousness. (1 John 1:9)

I confess my iniquity; I am troubled by my sin. (Psalms 38:18)

Therefore confess your sins to each other and pray for each other so that you may be healed. The prayer of a righteous person is powerful and effective. (James 5:16)

The Heart of Jesus for You

Jesus says: Don't let sin dwell underneath the surface of your life. Don't let it bubble away in the background. Don't say, "Tomorrow I'll sort it out." When Moses asked Pharaoh when he wanted to get rid of the plague of frogs, Pharaoh said tomorrow. He let his people suffer one more day rather than admit he was wrong and repent. Pride will enable sin to stay in your heart because you are afraid to be humble and ask for help. You still want to control things.

Get low and ask for help. Don't let the sin-stain remain within you. Humble yourself and be cleansed. Sin destroys. I give new life. Don't delay one more day. Confess and receive forgiveness and hope. I am your greatest treasure…

Thought

Ongoing sin in your life will quench the fire of God in you. If you sin, are you still a Christian? Yes. If you sin, are you still loved by the Lord? Yes. If you sin, will you lose your spiritual passion? Yes. I urge you to look at your life and see if there is any ongoing sin in your life. A Puritan in the 17th century called John Owen said: "Be killing sin or it will be killing you."

Do not put off until tomorrow what you need to put to death today. Don't be like Pharaoh, who subjected himself and all his people to one more night of misery. Why did he say to Moses to get rid of the frogs tomorrow? Why didn't he say get rid of them right now! It was pride, one last thing he could control in the face of the Almighty God even though everyone suffered. That's what sin does. It makes you suffer. It makes people around you suffer. Let's be honest. We normally sin because it is enjoyable. If it wasn't enjoyable then we wouldn't do it. We need to realise that Jesus is our greatest treasure and the greatest comfort we could ever have.

In Revelation, the angels and archangels and all the company of Heaven are crying out: 'Holy, holy, holy, worthy is the Lamb that was slain.' (Rev 4:8) That's your Jesus. Without Him you are lost. With Him you have everything. He is your greatest treasure, and sin in your life will disrupt that relationship. Put to death that ongoing sin in your life today and don't wait until tomorrow. The journey of faith will be too difficult if you don't.

What is Jesus saying to you?

27. LEAN

Scripture

Trust in the LORD with all your heart and lean not on your own understanding; in all your ways submit to him, and he will make your paths straight. (Proverbs 3:5-6)

Some trust in chariots and some in horses, but we trust in the name of the LORD our God. (Psalms 20:7)

May the God of hope fill you with all joy and peace as you trust in him, so that you may overflow with hope by the power of the Holy Spirit. (Romans 15:13)

The Heart of Jesus for You

Jesus says: I am the source of all joy. I am the source of all happiness. Any joy or happiness outside of me is temporary and inferior to the joy and happiness that I can give you. Leaning on your own understanding can be a blockage to my joy and happiness. It can twist your perception of what I am doing to the point that you don't think I'm doing anything. When that happens any joy you had disappears in the funnel of frustration and fear. Trust me with all of your heart. Surrender daily and in that surrender you will once again find freedom and joy. Open your heart and release the cares that you have and let me place in your empty hands the gifts that I want to give you. In doing that you'll be able to rejoice and be glad in every season of life…

Thought

On the 28th of October 1978 I was baptised by full immersion in a Plymouth Brethren church in Hamilton, Scotland. I was 14 years old. As a gift, my parents gave me a little leather RSV Bible, which I still have. Inside it, written in beautiful calligraphy, was Proverbs 3:5-6, a verse that I have held onto since then.

Many times since that day, I have given the act of leaning on my own understanding a real good go. I became pretty expert at it. Each time though, I reached a place where I realised that my own understanding was incredibly broken, weak and fallible. I once again learnt that the journey of faith was about simply learning to trust in the Lord with all of my heart.

- Leaning on your own understanding brings anxiety
- Trusting in the Lord with all your heart brings peace
- Leaning on your own understanding reduces joy
- Trusting in the Lord with all your heart increases his joy
- Leaning on your own understanding depletes faith
- Trusting in the Lord with all your heart releases faith to you and to others.

So, lean on the Lord, not on yourself or your own understanding. Hand over your understanding of things to God, open your empty hands and surrender to him in trust.

What is Jesus saying to you?

28. GRAIN

Scripture

Very truly I tell you, unless a kernel of wheat falls to the ground and dies, it remains only a single seed. But if it dies, it produces many seeds. (John 12:24)

Then he said to them all: "Whoever wants to be my disciple must deny themselves and take up their cross daily and follow me. For whoever wants to save their life will lose it, but whoever loses their life for me will save it. What good is it for someone to gain the whole world, and yet lose or forfeit their very self? Whoever is ashamed of me and my words, the Son of Man will be ashamed of them when he comes in his glory and in the glory of the Father and of the holy angels. (Luke 9:21-33)

The Heart of Jesus for You

Jesus says: Unless a grain of wheat falls to the ground and dies, it will not produce fruit. The cost of discipleship is death to self in order that you may receive life from me. Death can be frightening. The thought of surrendering all can be terrifying, but I will not forsake you or let you down. The thought of letting you down never enters my mind. It can look "un-sensible" to follow me from a worldly standpoint. People may say you are silly or naive. People may say you are being irresponsible to give it all up, to give everything away. They may say that you are not thinking of your children or family. Do you think that I don't love your children and family? Do you not think that I care for them as much as you do, or even more than you do? I have a better plan for your children than you do. The safest place for you all is the centre of my will, no matter how strange that looks. Do you not think that what you are doing may be the catalyst for revolution and revelations in your children's and family's lives? I am the Lord of the Harvest...

Thought

Dietrich Bonhoeffer wrote[4]: "Cheap grace is the preaching of forgiveness without repentance, baptism without church discipline, communion without confession,

---

[4] Cost of Discipleship, Dietrich Bonhoeffer, Chapter 1

absolution without personal confession. Cheap grace is grace without discipleship, grace without the cross, grace without Jesus Christ living and incarnate."

Cheap grace abounds in Christianity today. Very few are prepared to pay the cost of discipleship. Jesus said: 'Whoever wants to be my disciple must deny themselves and take up their cross daily and follow me. Whoever wants to save their life will lose it, but whoever loses their life for me will save it.' (Luke 9:23-24)

If you are on this journey of faith to start a great ministry then you can forget it. It is not about your ministry. It is all about Jesus and if our lives are not laid down in complete surrender, even to death, then we are on this journey for the wrong reason. Today, bow before the mighty king and declare: 'I want to be a coin in your pocket for you to spend any way you want. I want your glory to rest on me. I want to be the donkey you ride on. I just want to be yielded[5].'

What is Jesus saying to you?

---

[5] Randy Clark, Pressing in - Spend and be spent, Chapter 1

29. HOPE

Scripture

May integrity and uprightness protect me, because my hope, LORD, is in you. (Psalms 25:21)

Be strong and take heart, all you who hope in the LORD. (Psalms 31:24)

To them God has chosen to make known among the Gentiles the glorious riches of this mystery, which is Christ in you, the hope of glory. (Colossians 1:27)

The Heart of Jesus for You

Jesus says: Do not lose heart and do not lose hope. For I have overcome the world. In the midst of nothing seeming to happen, worship me. When you do, inertia will be transformed into momentum and that momentum will be unstoppable. It takes a lot of tenacity and perseverance to overcome inertia. Not that you make the movement happen, but you are ready to respond with hope and faithfulness to the slightest movement of my Spirit. That is faith and I'm going to give you more faith as a gift. Receive it right now. You cannot manufacture faith. Faith comes from me and I gladly and freely impart more to you. Continue to be tenacious and continue to persevere. The next movement is here. Be alert to my presence in conversations and connections and do not lose heart or hope…

Thought

According to Wikipedia[6]: 'Inertia is the resistance of any physical object to change in its velocity.' Inertia comes from the Latin word in 'iners' meaning idle or sluggish. Momentum[7] is 'the force that keeps an object moving.' If you increase mass or velocity then you increase your momentum. Spiritually speaking, more of God in your life, then more spiritual momentum. Momentum is changed, positively or negatively, normally in some sort of collision, where an object is slowed or sped up, or the direction of it is changed.

Life is full of collisions. Events happen that take us by

---

[6] https://en.wikipedia.org/wiki/Inertia

[7] https://dictionary.cambridge.org/dictionary/english/momentum

surprise. Decisions are made that can affect us negatively. Doors close that we thought we were meant to walk through. Occurrences, such as these, can affect our spiritual momentum. We find ourselves going in a different direction and we are unsure how to get back onto the narrow path. Or, we find that we have gone into reverse spiritually and are walking further and further away from Jesus. He is our hope, so we are walking away from hope. The incredible truth is that God, in his mercy, comes down to you. He has his hand upon you. He is in control, despite it looking as though everything is out of control. He is hope. He is mercy. He is grace. He is worthy of our praise whatever the season, so bow your head and give thanks to the God who has rescued you, who will rescue you and who is recusing you. And then wait for hope to draw near.

What is Jesus saying to you?

30. BEES

Scripture

Indeed, we felt we had received the sentence of death. But this happened that we might not rely on ourselves but on God, who raises the dead. (2 Corinthians 1:9)

Put on the full armour of God, so that you can take your stand against the Devil's schemes. (Ephesians 6:11)

Be alert and of sober mind. Your enemy the Devil prowls around like a roaring lion looking for someone to devour. (1 Peter 5:8)

The Heart of Jesus for You

Jesus says: The attack of your spiritual enemy can be like a swarm of bees attacking from every direction and you feel powerless to stop them. As soon as you swat one bee, another is already attacking you. No matter how strong you are you may feel overwhelmed and discouraged. But I am coming in a glory cloud to placate the enemy and put it to sleep, so that you can trample on the enemy as you walk forward. Just like a beekeeper uses smoke to placate bees and make them docile, so my glory cloud will put your enemy to sleep and make it docile and sleepy. It will be easy for you to defeat the enemy. You may ask why I didn't come sooner, why I let you get stung. It was for two reasons. First, to show you that you cannot do this by yourself. Trials and afflictions are to make you rely more on me rather than your own strength. Second, to build your strength, determination and perseverance. You will be much fuller of faith and determination to continue than before. I am coming in my glory cloud…

Thought

On the faith journey there seem to be seasons when spiritual attacks are relentless. It may not be major attacks. It may be minor things, but as soon as you deal with one thing, another suddenly appears. It is as though a swarm of bees is attacking you and you run away, waving your hands in the air to try and get rid of them. To no avail. If you are in that season here are one or two suggestions:

1. Stand: "Therefore put on the full armour of God, so that when the day of evil comes, you may be able to stand

your ground, and after you have done everything, to stand." (Ephesians 6:13) To stand we can do various things. For example, put on worship, pray, etc. However, there will come a time when your most powerful spiritual weapon is simply to stand. Standing as followers of Jesus frightens the enemy.

2. Remember, there are more for you than against you. An army with horses and chariots surrounded Elisha and his servant. Elisha responds: "Open his eyes, LORD, so that he may see." Then the LORD opened the servant's eyes, and he looked and saw the hills full of horses and chariots of fire all around Elisha." (2 Kings 6: 17) God is with you and you are in the majority and on the side of victory, even though it doesn't feel like it sometimes. May the Lord open your eyes to see the mighty army of God that surrounds you and is with you.

What is Jesus saying to you?

31. WAVES

Scripture

For no matter how many promises God has made, they are "Yes" in Christ. And so through him the "Amen" is spoken by us to the glory of God. (2 Corinthians 1:20)

And we know that in all things God works for the good of those who love him, who have been called according to his purpose. (Romans 8:28)

The Heart of Jesus for You

Jesus says: It can feel like you're being tossed from wave to wave and that you are constantly submerged under rough seas. Each time you surface to get some air, another wave comes crashing down upon you and you feel helplessly rolled about underwater. You are tired and aching, but please hear me: all is not lost, this is not the end. I am using the storms of life to throw you onto your paradise island. You may ask me if there was an easier way. There are easier ways, but they don't make you as strong and as resilient as this way does. And here is a challenging part: give thanks in the middle of being thrown around in the storms. It is a sweet fragrance to me. It is beautiful and it will soften your heart. Your paradise island is near. Trust me. When fear and doubt are assailing you, you must stand on the promises that have been made. Read the promises in Scripture. All the promises of God the Father are YES in me. The promises are YES to you. Read again the prophetic words and let them encourage you. My breath is within you. I am your oxygen tank when you are submerged…

Thought

It is easy to criticise Peter for sinking after taking his eyes of Jesus, but what about all the other disciples who were still in the boat? They didn't step out in faith and walk on water. Peter did and, even though he sank, he took a step of faith. When he was in the boat, in the middle of the storm, I think Peter realised the safest place in the storm was to be near Jesus.

In our journey of faith it can feel like we are being tossed from wave to wave. It can seem that we are getting nowhere and we get exhausted. But, perhaps like Peter, you have stepped out of the boat and taken a step of faith. The Lord will not let you down. In fact, he may be using the waves of the storms to drive you to the place he wants you to be. It may be that the currents of the ocean storms are propelling you to where God's intended place for you. As Puritan Thomas Case[8] writes: "God can use the Devil's weapons and devices to beat him. God will defeat the Devil with his own weapons." All things work for good to those who love and serve the Lord.

What is Jesus saying to you?

---

[8] Voices from the Past, Edited by Richard Rushing, Banner of Truth, 2009, p325

32. RESPONSE

Scripture

Keep me free from the trap that is set for me, for you are my refuge. Into your hands I commit my spirit; deliver me, LORD, my faithful God. (Psalm 31:4-5)

They were using this question as a trap, in order to have a basis for accusing him. But Jesus bent down and started to write on the ground with his finger. (John 8:6)

The Heart of Jesus for You

Jesus says: No weapon formed against you shall prosper. Even though those who are against you may attempt to trap you in meetings or seemingly harmless decisions, I have placed within you a discernment alarm that will go off when the enemy is in action. Listen to my voice when you are in meetings, discussions and conversations. Let me guide you and give strength for the journey and the decisions you have to make. Do not become suspicious of people who disagree with you. You need people who disagree with you and love you. It is iron sharpening iron. As you follow my steps, you will be led around the traps set for you and those who created them and set them will fall into them instead. Do not rejoice in that, as I love those who are trying to trap you and disrupt your journey. Instead, pray for my blessing to be upon them. Then offence will not enter your heart…

Thought

One of the gifts of the Holy Spirit is the gift of discernment. According to the Merrian-Webster dictionary, discernment is the quality of being able to grasp and comprehend what is obscure. It is recognising hidden motives. Some people may have an increased natural ability to do that, but for the followers of Jesus we look to the Holy Spirit to give us the gift of discernment.

The gift of discernment is the ability to appraise a situation from God's perspective and hear His voice on the matter in order to tell what is really going on. AW Tozer[9] said: 'Among the gifts of the Spirit, scarcely one is of greater practical usefulness than the gift of discernment.

---

[9] https://quotessayings.net/topics/the-spirit-of-discernment/

This gift should be highly valued and frankly sought as being almost indispensable in these critical times. This gift will enable us to distinguish the chaff from the wheat and to divide the manifestation of the flesh from the operation of the Spirit.'

On your journey of faith cry out for the gift of discernment. It may not be that people are trying to trap you, but that you have to make a choice or a response to a situation or someone. Discernment will open your eyes to the spiritual realm and the hearts and desires of those around you. You will be able to see things others cannot yet see and you can take steps of faith with those discernment insights. Pray for the gift of discernment.

What is Jesus saying to you?

33. RESTING

Scripture

But Martha was distracted by all the preparations that had to be made. She came to him and asked, "Lord, don't you care that my sister has left me to do the work by myself? Tell her to help me!" "Martha, Martha," the Lord answered, "you are worried and upset about many things, but few things are needed—or indeed only one. Mary has chosen what is better, and it will not be taken away from her." (Luke 10:40-42)

But Stephen, full of the Holy Spirit, looked up to Heaven and saw the glory of God, and Jesus standing at the right hand of God. (Acts 7:55)

The Heart of Jesus for You

Jesus says: Do not strive to make a right standing with me or to make the future happen. Striving is a sign of a lack of faith. You may feel that you have to do as much as you can to get to where you think I want you to go, as though it depends on you. Do you think I am unable to work out my plans in your life? What I want you to work on is resting in me, surrendering all to me. That is the safest and the most fruitful place you can be. It doesn't mean to say that you will be in an easy place. What it does mean is that you will know peace and joy in each and every circumstance. Your lack of striving will puzzle people as they see how restful and fruitful you are. You are doing the one thing necessary. You don't have to strive and be like other people. This is not about being lazy or not working hard. This is about striving. Striving in yourself and resting in me are diametrically opposed. One is about you taking control of your life. One is about trusting in me with your life. The only striving you should do is to do good to other people...

Thought

When nothing seems to be happening or opening up it can be tempting to try and make something happen. We may not even be aware that we are doing that. We have all tried to force doors to open. It is exhausting and tiring to do that. A friend of mine used a little phrase that I love:

118

Push and Pray. You should not push without praying and you should not pray without pushing. If we just push doors all of the time without praying we are living from a worldly point of view. If you just pray all the time without pushing then you are not being proactive. You need to push and pray. Security for the future does not come from a job or a role. It comes from the Lord. He is the safest place!

Faith is letting God do what He wants and letting Him direct your steps. Faith is living the story to which you don't know the ending. That is where peace comes from and it is much more fun to let Him lead. That is true freedom and true awakening. As the Graham Kendrick song says: 'Let me do my work among you, do not strive, do not strive. Let my peace reign within your heart, do not strive, do not strive.'

What is Jesus saying to you?

34. PEOPLE

Scripture

And let us consider how we may spur one another on toward love and good deeds, not giving up meeting together, as some are in the habit of doing, but encouraging one another—and all the more as you see the Day approaching. (Hebrews 10:24-25)

Psalms 133

How good and pleasant it is

when God's people live together in unity!

It is like precious oil poured on the head,

running down on the beard,

running down on Aaron's beard,

down on the collar of his robe.

It is as if the dew of Hermon

were falling on Mount Zion.

For there the LORD bestows his blessing,

even life forevermore.

The Heart of Jesus for You

Jesus says: Love my people well. It will be very easy to find some reasons not to love them well. They can be stubborn and frustrating, but so can you and I love you very well. Make a choice to be present to each person that is talking to you. See them as a child of God, your brother or sister. Don't look over them or around them as they talk, seeing if there is someone else to talk to. Focus on them. The few moments of you taking the time to listen to them could be the very thing that they need at that moment. Many times those who are not seen as "worthy" in the world's eyes have not been listened to for a long time. They have a voice and they have something to say, something to contribute. Maybe what they say to you will be a prophetic word for your life. How will you know if you don't take a few moments to listen to them? Love my people well...

Thought

People can be so infuriating! There can be many reasons not to love others, to distance ourselves from them. In a C.S. Lewis book, called 'The Great Divorce', Hell is portrayed as people being increasingly distanced from one another, isolated and alone. According to CS Lewis, separation is the essential idea of Hell. You may sometimes think that being with others is not like Heaven at all, but that is a big feature of Heaven. Community. That is why it's called the church, a gathering.

Community is 'life together' to use the Dietrich Bonhoeffer phrase. On the journey of faith you need to be with other people, you need to be in community with followers of Jesus. Don't make the excuse that it is impossible for you to do that. If you can't get with others physically, use Zoom, FaceTime or Skype. If you have withdrawn from people, you really need to reconnect. In one location we stayed, the local church was a liturgical Anglican Church, no musicians and 15 people. The worship music was an organ on a backing track. But it was the people of God and we needed to be there. Love people well and be present for them.

What is Jesus saying to you?

35. REMEMBER

Scripture

Be careful that you do not forget the LORD, who brought you out of Egypt, out of the land of slavery. (Deuteronomy 6:12)

Praise the LORD, my soul,

and forget not all his benefits (Psalms 103:2)

I will never forget your precepts,

for by them you have preserved my life. (Psalms 119:93)

The Heart of Jesus for You

Jesus says: Remember all that I have done for you before. It can seem at times that I have forgotten about you or that I have abandoned you. I have not and I never will. When I said that I would be with my followers always, I meant it as truth and not just a nice final phrase to my ministry on Earth. Part of the reason for this season is to enable your faith to grow stronger and to rely on me more and more. Many times when I don't seem to be present, people try to work out things for themselves. That is not the way to go. Respond to my prompting and not to the desperation of wanting something to happen. The way through this time is very simple: remember. Remember all that I have done. Remember the previous miracles. Remember the past provision. Remember my power and who I am. I have done it before and I will do it again. My unseen steps are leading you to where I want you to go. Follow me...

Thought

I recall my parents telling me a story of their faith walk. In the 1970's we would go as a family to Italy for six to eight weeks during the summer to do outreach. My parents would take teams of young people from Scotland and they would give out Christian literature and lead gospel missions with local Italian churches. One year, we were in Salerno, south of Naples. My parents, my two brothers and myself had driven down from Glasgow in a VW caravanette. I can remember it was orange. The first team of young people had come and gone and we were waiting for the second group to fly out. My parents realised that they did not have any money to buy petrol to get back to Scotland. No mobiles, no internet banking. Just raw faith. The next group arrived and one of the girls gave my parents an envelope with a letter and money inside. Someone in their Plymouth Brethren church had felt a prompting of the Lord to send money to them without knowing the situation. It was enough to buy petrol for the journey home. That is my faith heritage.

I will not forget that story of faith, and many others. It constantly reminds me that I am walking on a path of faith on which my parents, and many others, have walked. Do not forget all that the Lord has done. Write them in a journal and give the Lord thanks for the history you have with God.

Puritan John Flavel[10] writes: "Be careful that you do not forget the kind provision God has graciously supplied in the past and do not murmur and regret under new straits." He continues: "There is a dangerous influence in fullness in most men to forget God." Remember!

---

[10] Voices from the Past, Banner of Truth

What is Jesus saying to you?

36. SITUATION

Scripture

Trust in the LORD with all your heart and lean not on your own understanding; in all your ways submit to him, and he will make your paths straight. (Proverbs 3:5-6)

Jesus replied, "Truly I tell you, if you have faith and do not doubt, not only can you do what was done to the fig tree, but also you can say to this mountain, 'Go, throw yourself into the sea,' and it will be done. (Matthew 21:21)

The Heart of Jesus for You

Jesus says: Do not lean on your own understanding. Trust in my Father to guide you in each situation. When times and situations are difficult and people are against you, fear can enter your heart. When fear enters your heart there is a tendency to control situations and people, instead of releasing things to me. Fear leads to control. Faith leads to freedom. When you are fearful you want to make snap decisions in the heat of the fear. Do not do that. That is leaning on your own understanding. Trust in my Father.

Look up to Him. Lean on the Holy Spirit. Cast all your cares on me. Do not make any decision until you have come to us in prayer. Seek our heart for the situation. In all situations, in all your goings on, acknowledge us as Lord and we will direct your paths…

Thought

We can face many different situations on our faith journey. What is our response to those situations? Often, I suspect, it can be fear, and fear can lead to doubt and, maybe even, despair.

In 'The Pilgrim's Progress,' Christian and his companion 'Hopeful' wander from the path that they were supposed to stay on. They find themselves imprisoned in Doubting Castle. The castle is run by 'Giant Despair'. He starves his prisoners and tries to convince them to end their lives. He beats them after being counselled by his wife, who was called 'Diffidence'. He said to them: 'For why would you carry on living when it is so painful?'

They begin to pray and continue all night in prayer, even though they are despairing. Christian discovers a key and the key was called 'Promise'. The key opened the door to their jail and they escaped and went back on the narrow path, the one they had been told to walk on.

Maybe you have felt despair. Maybe you have wandered from the narrow path. Maybe you have wondered what options are left to you. Do not despair and let hope speak into your life. Come to the Lord with all of your burdens and offload them onto Him. You will also, like Christian, find the key called 'Promise' that will lead you into freedom. All of God's promises are 'YES" in Jesus! Don't try to work it all out. Trust in Him!

What is Jesus saying to you?

37. UNDIVIDED

Scripture

Don't let anyone look down on you because you are young, but set an example for the believers in speech, in conduct, in love, in faith and in purity. (1 Timothy 4:12)

All who have this hope in him purify themselves, just as he is pure. (1 John 3:3)

The Heart of Jesus for You

Jesus says: Let your heart be undivided. Let it be solely focused on me and don't sit on the fence. I am all you need. I am your greatest comfort. I am your greatest hope. Lead others to me by the way you live and they will find me and their healing. You do not need to try and fix them. Love them and lead them to me. It can seem as though the world is getting crazier and weirder and that the church is getting more and more lukewarm. Do not worry. I am coming to face people, to face the church, and to confront them with a decision to follow me or not. I am coming in revival and not everyone will want it as it will change the way that they live - even Christians will get offended by revival. Offence happens when your will and your ways are not accepted. But I am asking you to accept my way and my thoughts, which are higher than yours. Do not lose hope or get discouraged by what you see, for I am working in the world for the glory of my Father. Let your heart be undivided...

Thought

James, in his typically direct manner, says: 'Wash your hands you sinners and purify your heart, you double minded.' (James 4:8) Purity can also be described as being undivided. It is being willing to put to death spiritually and daily, the things that would split our hearts wide open and lead us away from the Lord. This is a daily battle and I must not get discouraged.

I want to highlight three verses in Scripture:

1. Have an undivided heart: '"Remember, LORD, how I have walked before you faithfully and with wholehearted devotion and have done what is good in your eyes." And Hezekiah wept bitterly.' (2 Kings 20:3) The NIV has the

phrase 'wholehearted devotion'. The ESV has 'whole heart'. This talks of our motives for what we do. Everything we do is to bring glory to the Lord.

2. Have an undivided loyalty: '...experienced soldiers prepared for battle with every type of weapon, to help David with undivided loyalty.' (1 Chronicles 12:33) The context of this is of a battle. An army cannot function if there is no loyalty. It is also true within the church, the Lord's Army. Choose to be loyal.

3. Have an undivided mind: 'Teach me your way, LORD, and I will live by your truth. Give me an undivided mind to fear your name.' (Psalm 86:11, Christian Standard Bible). This touches our 'Finally, brothers and sisters, whatever is true, whatever is noble, whatever is right, whatever is pure, whatever is lovely, whatever is admirable—if anything is excellent or praiseworthy—think about such things.(Philippians 4:8)

Do not be afraid to stand firm for the truth with an undivided heart, mind and loyalty. Be a pure stream.

What is Jesus saying to you?

38. LIGHT

Scripture

Arise, shine, for your light has come, and the glory of the LORD rises upon you. See, darkness covers the Earth and thick darkness is over the peoples, but the LORD rises upon you and his glory appears over you. Nations will come to your light, and kings to the brightness of your dawn. (Isaiah 60:1-3)

The light shines in the darkness, and the darkness has not overcome it. (John 1:5)

The Heart of Jesus for You

Jesus says: Let my light shine out of you. You are a light on a hill. You are the salt of the Earth. You are not to condemn, but to love others deeply and not to compromise. Grace and truth. It is a balance to love and not to compromise. It is a narrow road that you are called to walk on. When you are in difficult situations and conversations I will give you the words to say. I will not abandon you, but I will be with you. Turn around. Look in a different direction and you will see me. Light brings joy and security. Be joyful in every circumstance. Bring my truth and do not worry about people's reactions. Truth riles and disturbs, as people want to go on their own way and they want to justify what they are doing in their lifestyle choices. Do not be surprised when people come against you. Do not judge them. My Father is the judge. Be salt and light...

Thought

One Sunday evening I was walking to church. It was winter and so it was very dark. We were in a little village in Dorset and I was walking in country lanes with high hedgerows and no street lights. It was pitch black. I had a little torch and it wasn't very powerful, but as soon as I put it on the darkness disappeared and I felt courage rise even though all around me was inky blackness.

It can sometimes seem that we are weak, little torches in an oppressive darkness. But we make a difference. Can you imagine if someone was walking on the same country lane that I was walking on, but they didn't have a torch?

How glad would they be to walk alongside someone with light? Sometimes, it can be different though. Maybe the same person is walking towards you, without a torch, and you shine the light in their face. The reaction might be a different one, maybe one of anger at being blinded. People will react differently to the light shining in and through you. Some will be pleased and some will get angry.

As I was walking along that country lane a car came up behind me, headlights blazing. My little torch light disappeared in comparison to the car headlights. Jesus is the blazing sun in whose glory we walk.

What is Jesus saying to you?

39. CLOSENESS

Scripture

And surely I am with you always, to the very end of the age. (Matthew 28:20)

Be strong and courageous. Do not be afraid or terrified because of them, for the LORD your God goes with you; he will never leave you nor forsake you. (Deuteronomy 31:6)

The Heart of Jesus for You

Jesus says: I have never left you, even for a moment, for I am your Saviour, not one who abandons. I came down to Earth, I do not walk away from it. I do not destroy you, but I do destroy the works of the evil one. I do not punish, I teach. I said to my disciples that I would be with them - and you - always. Those were not empty words, but a truth that I still practice today. Your feelings can be deceptive and tell you things that are not true. You may not feel my closeness, but I can assure you that I am so near to you and that I will not leave you. Cast your cares upon me and flee from sin...

Thought

Jesus saves. He doesn't neglect or abandon. He is the great Shepherd, who searches for the one sheep that was lost. As Jesus ascended into Heaven he said to disciples - and that includes us - that he will be with us always. He is with us always through the presence of the Holy Spirit in our lives.

Sometimes, we don't feel the closeness of the Lord because of choices that we make. James challenges us: 'Come near to God and he will come near to you.' (James 4:8) The chorus says, 'Turn your eyes upon Jesus and look full in his wonderful face, and the things of Earth will grow strangely dim, in the light of His glory and grace.'

Sometimes, we don't feel the closeness of the Lord because we are looking at, or concentrating on, the wrong thing or looking in the wrong direction. Once, in Scotland when I was 17 or 18 years old, I had an encounter with a demonic presence. I was walking along the corridor of a big house, where I was attending a young people's camp. All of a sudden, I felt a hand on my shoulder. Not an imaginary hand, but a real hand. I looked around and no one was there.   I had an overwhelming sense of something ungodly. My parents, who were helping to lead the camp, had led a witch to the Lord and I believe the Devil was trying to bring harm to my parents through me. I was terrified and ran to the kitchen, where my parents were. My mum gave me a Bible and I threw it against the wall aggressively saying I didn't want that.

Forward nearly 40 years. I was being prayed for at Bethel Church, Redding. The couple asked me to think of that moment as they prayed. I was scared. They asked me to look around at the scene in my mind's eye. I did so, and as I turned my head (something I've never done before as I was so fixated on where I had felt the hand) Jesus was standing beside me with his hand upon my other shoulder. He had been there all that time. For 40 years. I had just never seen him, as I had focused on the work of the enemy. Turn your eyes and discover Jesus in your situation.

What is Jesus saying to you?

40. HOME

Scripture

The LORD said to Moses, "Speak to the Israelites and say to them: 'After you enter the land I am giving you as a home." (Numbers 15:1-2)

How lovely is your dwelling place, LORD Almighty! My soul yearns, even faints, for the courts of the LORD; my heart and my flesh cry out for the living God. Even the sparrow has found a home, and the swallow a nest for herself, where she may have her young— a place near your altar, LORD Almighty, my King and my God. (Psalm 84:1-3)

The Heart of Jesus for You

Jesus says: I am your home, your place of rest, your place of safety and refreshment. I am the door, by which you enter your home. I am the light, by which you see in your home. I am the bread, which you eat in your home. I am your security, by which you feel safe in your home. I am the still water, where you find rest in your home. I am the way to your home. I am the life in your home. I am the truth, by which you find your home. I will give you clothes that will never wear out in your home. I am the power source for your home. I am the cornerstone of your home. Come and enter and find peace and rest from your weary journey. I am your home. Welcome home...

Thought

Jan and I went through a long season of homelessness. We didn't live on the street, but we didn't own a home and have had to rely on the provision of the Lord and the generosity of people to house us. It really gives you an appreciation of home.

Home brings stability, not only to you, but to your whole family. However, homes can be lost. Money can disappear. Jobs can be gone. Security is not to be found in these things. Our true home is God. For 40 years the children of Israel wandered in the desert and moved 41 times in that time. It must have been exhausting. Oh, but the miracles they saw during that time! The parting of the Red Sea. Water coming from a rock. Birds flying into the camp to be eaten. Angel bread falling from Heaven every day. Clothes and shoes that did not wear out. I cannot think of any other miracles like that in Scripture that happened for a nation. In that time, I believe they began to learn that God was their home. As long as the pillar of fire and the pillar of cloud were present they knew that the Lord was there. In our season of homelessness we experienced things that we experienced before God's provision in an unprecedented way. But the most important lesson we learnt is that God is our home, even if we have to keep moving.

What is Jesus saying to you?

41. MAP

Scripture

"Call to me and I will answer you and tell you great and unsearchable things you do not know." (Jeremiah 33:3)

As for God, his way is perfect: The LORD'S word is flawless; he shields all who take refuge in him. (Psalms 18:30)

Jesus answered, "I am the way and the truth and the life. No one comes to the Father except through me." (John 14:6)

The Heart of Jesus for You

Jesus says: If you have lost your way, then I am your map. Call my name and it will bring to mind all of the truth that you have forgotten. Call my name and your heart will be jump-started into beating for me once again. Call on my name and I will direct your paths as you trust in me with all your heart and as you stop leaning on your own understanding. Even when you are off the narrow path I will come and find you. When you have fallen into a pit, I will pull you out of it, if you repent and give me your hand and trust in me again. You do not need to be lost or stuck anymore. Call on me and I will answer you and show you great and unsearchable things that you do not know…

Thought

One of the most natural reactions when you are lost is to call out. 'Hello, is anyone there?', you may shout. You just need to know the safety of not being alone and having someone near, who can help you find your way.

It is easy to lose your way on the journey of faith. As I mentioned before, the story of the 'Pilgrim's Progress' is a helpful picture of that. We can lose our way for various reasons, deliberate or non-deliberate sin; loss of faith in what the Lord is supposed to be doing; family issues; lack of a quiet time and many more. It may happen, but what is so important is that we do everything possible to get back onto the narrow way of faith.

Jeremiah was confused and the people of God lost their way. The Lord said to Jeremiah: 'Call to me and I will answer you and tell you great and unsearchable things you do not know.' (Jeremiah 33:3).

This verse tell us several helpful things:

1. God does not turn His back on His people - that is you.

2. If we call, He will answer us.

3. We discover it is not about us – God will tell us things we couldn't possibly discover.

4. Revelation is near.

If I feel lost, I just start to call out the name of Jesus over and over. I always discover he comes and finds me again and again. Call Jesus today.

What is Jesus saying to you?

42. COURAGE

Scripture

But Jesus immediately said to them: "Take courage! It is I. Don't be afraid." (Matthew 14:27)

I eagerly expect and hope that I will in no way be ashamed, but will have sufficient courage so that now as always Christ will be exalted in my body, whether by life or by death. (Philippians 1:20)

The Heart of Jesus for You

Jesus says: Hold on and do not give up. Do not give into discouragement which, as the name suggests, depletes your courage and so you become fearful, controlling and lacking in faith. I told Joshua, 'Be strong and very courageous' and I say the same to you as you enter the promised land, for you are standing at the border of a new land. It is in front of you, but it looks so different and unfamiliar to you that you are hesitating. Be strong and very courageous and step into all that is in front of you. Embrace that which I have spoken to you about. You have no lack, even if you do not have financial means in your bank account. Do you think I was intimidated when I was given five loaves and two fish to feed nearly 20,000 people? I can take the money in your bank account and multiply it to buy whatever is needed, including a home and property. So, do not lose heart and do not stop pursuing all that I have called you to do...

Thought

The task given to Joshua was huge. Taking over from a successful leader is always daunting. Moses was a spiritual giant, but remember his call at the burning bush. He tried to make excuses and in the end Aaron was his mouth pierce as he said he couldn't speak without stuttering. Not a promising start for a man who was going to be a spiritual giant.

Joshua probably felt the same as Moses did, and the Lord graciously spoke into his life: "Be strong and very courageous.

Walking the path of faith needs courage. When your bank account is empty and you do not know in which direction to go it can be scary. It can seem all very exciting to take a step of faith until you actually have to take a step of faith. Then it can be scary and you need courage. Think of Peter as he stepped out of the boat onto water. I suspect the waves seemed to be bigger out of the boat than when he was in it. But, by faith, you can walk this path. Do not think that the Lord has run out of ideas or resources. Do not think that He has been defeated in this situation. Do not think that this is the end of the road for you, even though you cannot see a way forward. This is an opportunity for God to be revealed as spectacular!

God's grace is sufficient for you. I know it is enough because I have experienced it in the most traumatic and difficult season I have been through. He will not fail you! Be strong and very courageous.

What is Jesus saying to you?

43. SURRENDER

Scripture

May God himself, the God of peace, sanctify you through and through. May your whole spirit, soul and body be kept blameless at the coming of our Lord Jesus Christ. (1 Thessalonians 5:23)

And whoever does not carry their cross and follow me cannot be my disciple. (Luke 14:27)

The Heart of Jesus for You

Jesus says: Will you surrender all? Many want salvation, but not sanctification. They want to be saved from destruction, but they don't want to give up the so-called pleasures of this world. You cannot have a divided heart. As I said to Peter: "Do you really love me?" Many people want the benefits of salvation, but they do not want to deny themselves and take up their cross. They want to be my disciples, but are not willing to pay the cost of discipleship. Oh, that you would surrender all and give me all of your heart. Nothing will be gained by sitting on the fence. In fact, it will be painful, since you have tasted and seen that I am good. Don't turn your back on my goodness. Let hope be your overriding emotion when you think of me. Let joy be your dominant feeling and enjoy my salvation as you pay the cost of discipleship…

Thought

Salvation is one thing. Being willing to be sanctified is another. Salvation is entering the Kingdom of God. Sanctification is being changed to live like Jesus in that Kingdom. Sanctification is the work of purification of a follower of Jesus in partnership with the Holy Spirit. James writes: "But someone will say, "You have faith; I have deeds." Show me your faith without deeds, and I will show you my faith by my deeds." (James 2:18)

I have found the process of daily surrender comes in stages. The first stage is the joy of surrender. We are excited by the thought of surrender and we genuinely want to give it all to Jesus. This is a genuine desire and it is good. This leads to the second stage, which is the battle of surrender. We are giving it all up joyfully and then reality hits. It's more difficult than we thought. Or sin rears its ugly head. Or our faith is simply not big enough yet. And so, we enter a battle. As we push through the second stage with the presence and joy of Jesus, and that might be a long process as the Holy Spirit helps us to grow our faith or purify our hearts, we will enter a third stage, which I call the peace of surrender. In this stage, we genuinely rest in Jesus and trust Him completely. From practical experience on the journey of faith, this is what I have found the process of surrender to be, with stage two being the longest. And it can be cyclical, or we can go back and forth between stages two and three. At some point we can be in the battle of surrender, and then we enter the peace of surrender for a short while after which we go back into the battle. You are not left alone. You can do this. Jesus is with you.

What is Jesus saying to you?

44. IRRATIONAL

Scripture

Do not be wise in your own eyes; fear the LORD and shun evil. (Proverbs 3:7)

Therefore everyone who hears these words of mine and puts them into practice is like a wise man who built his house on the rock. The rain came down, the streams rose, and the winds blew and beat against that house; yet it did not fall, because it had its foundation on the rock. (Matthew 7:24-25)

The Heart of Jesus for You

Jesus says: I will speak wisdom into your irrational fears. You are worrying about things that will probably never happen. You are imagining a worst case scenario, a picture of the future that is based on fear and conjecture. When has that ever been helpful to you? Instead, let me take the fear and give you a hope for the future. Again, I want to say that I have a greater plan for your family than you do and I have a greater love for them than you do.

Cultivate a learned optimism that is guided and shaped by the Holy Spirit and is based on faith rather than fear. Irrational fears are like sea anchors that will drag you down to the bottom of the ocean as other ships sail right above you. Hand over your irrational fears to me and trust in me with all of your heart…

Thought

Most of my fears never come to pass. Many of them are figments of my imagination. Most of them are based on what I think could possibly happen, but never do. Most of my fears are irrational. Why is it that we always imagine the worst case scenario is going to happen? Why don't we imagine the best case scenario is going to happen?

The Lord doesn't give us fears. It is not one of the gifts of the Spirit that He gives out. There is no gift of fear in Galatians or Corinthians. Instead, He gives us hope. He gives us faith. He gives us courage.

The writer of Hebrews writes: 'We have this hope as an anchor for the soul, firm and secure. It enters the inner sanctuary behind the curtain…' (Hebrews 6:19) The hope that Hebrews 6 refers to is the unchanging nature of the purposes of God, which He promised - 'Because God wanted to make the unchanging nature of his purpose very clear to the heirs of what was promised, he confirmed it with an oath.' (Hebrews 6:17) What we need in times of irrationality is an anchor to hold us steady.

Paul writes in Philippians 1:6: 'being confident of this, that he who began a good work in you will carry it on to completion until the day of Christ Jesus.' (Philippians 1:6). We can have absolute and total confidence in what God wants to do in and through us.

The opposite of irrationality is not rationality, but wisdom. To the world, what we do as followers of Jesus looks irrational, but it is wisdom to seek what the Lord's will is in any given situation. But what is rational to the world may not be God's wisdom for a situation.

Hand over all your irrationalities and irrational fears to the Lord and ask Him to give you a huge download of hope, faith and wisdom.

What is Jesus saying to you?

45. BUILD

Scripture

And I tell you that you are Peter, and on this rock I will build my church, and the gates of Hades will not overcome it. (Matthew 16:18)

On that day a great persecution broke out against the church in Jerusalem, and all except the apostles were scattered throughout Judea and Samaria….Those who had been scattered preached the word wherever they went. (Acts 8:1, 4)

His intent was that now, through the church, the manifold wisdom of God should be made known to the rulers and authorities in the Heavenly realms… (Ephesians 3:10)

The Heart of Jesus for You

Jesus says: I will build my church and the gates of Hell will not prevail against it. The church is not a fragile thing. It has me as its foundation and cornerstone. People will try to build conservatories and extensions that I have not given planning permission for. Ultimately, those conservatories and extensions will crumble, but the church that stands on me, the Rock, will not crumble. Stand firm, therefore, even when the waves of the pervading culture slam against you and criticise you. In that slamming, they are slamming against me. In that criticism, they are criticising me. There will be a massive revival of rediscovery of true identity and many will wake up as though they have been in a drugged sleep. The enemy put a fire blanket over much of the church to put out the spiritual fire. I am now taking that fire blanket off, so that the fire can once again ignite, as the Holy Spirit breathes on it. There will be much repentance and reconciliation. Though not all will wake up and repent I will build my church…

Thought

I think that we have this subliminal (or not so subliminal in some cases) thought that we can build God's church. When you think about it, the idea is quite silly. We are simply like a brick in a building. The brick does not build a building. A bricklayer does. He uses bricks to build.

We do not build the church.

Some people may build organisations that are church-like, but they are not the church. Only God builds the church. 'Unless the Lord builds the house, the builders labour in vain.' (Psalm 127:1) Jesus said he would build his church, so let's ask him how it should be built.

For those of you wondering if what you are doing is worth it, as you tread the path of faith take the pressure off yourself of having to make something happen that looks remotely successful. Jesus will do the work. He uses us and works through us, which is our incredible privilege, but He is the one who makes it happen. If what happens through you is small, give thanks that He is working in your situation. We do not need business cards or social media accounts or the internet or smoke machines or big sound systems or fancy websites or even a building to build the church. We just need Jesus.

What is Jesus saying to you?

46. OVERCOME

Scripture

Immediately the boy's father exclaimed, "I do believe; help me overcome my unbelief!" (Mark 9:24)

You, God, are my God, earnestly I seek you; I thirst for you, my whole being longs for you, in a dry and parched land where there is no water. (Psalm 63:1)

The Heart of Jesus for You

Jesus says: I have overcome the world. The world has not overcome me. There can be times when it looks like my truth has been overcome. It has not. There will always be a remnant of faithful people, who will stand through truth no matter what comes against them. Do not be afraid when people oppose you, ostracise you or ridicule you. I am with you and I will give you the words to say and the strength to carry on. Persecution is the fertiliser of growth. Persecution brings life to dormant seeds, it wakes them up. Persecution can bring fruitfulness. Do not forget who I am. I am not some little demi-god. I am utterly the Lord of the universe! There is no other God apart from me and I am for you and not against you. I cut through space and time for you and my purpose will be fulfilled in you and through you. I have overcome the world...

Thought

You are an overcomer because the Holy Spirit lives in you, not because you are strong. To be filled, however, we can position ourselves and prepare our hearts. The letters to the churches in the book of Revelation, helps us in this. After the letter to each church there is a refrain: 'to the one who overcomes' (ESV)

1. The church in Ephesus: They are encouraged for their perseverance and for the fact that they have not grown weary. However, the Lord challenges them that they have lost their first love. The Ephesians are promised eternal life if they overcome (victorious, NIV). They will eat from the tree of life. Question: are you desperate for God?

2. The church in Smyrna: This church is encouraged for its endurance under affliction and that they have spiritual riches. They are slandered, but God speaks only good over

them. The overcomers will not be hurt by the second death, they will not go to Hell. Question: how will you endure under affliction?

3. The church in Pergamum: This church is commended for its faithfulness. They are in a spiritually bankrupt city, but they remain faithful even though it costs. But some of them hold to heresy and commit sexual immorality. If they repent they will be right with the Lord and become overcomers. If they overcome, they will experience supernatural provision and a new identity. Question: faithful Christian, is there anything in your life that you need to repent of?

4. The church in Thyatira: The church is commended for its love and faith and the fact that they persevere. Yet they tolerate immorality and idolatry. The one who overcomes will have authority over the nations. Question: are you tolerating anything spiritually that needs to be put to death?

5. The church in Sardis: Generally, the church is sleeping with only a few who have not compromised. Again, there is a call to repent. The one who overcomes

will be clothed in white and have their name in the book of life. Question: are you sleeping spiritually?

6. The church in Philadelphia: The Philadelphian church refused to deny the name of Jesus. As a result, the Lord presented them with an open door that no-one could shut. This church is called patiently to endure and they will be overcomers. They will be made a pillar in the temple of God and will continually worship the Lord. Question: how is your daily time with the Lord?

7. The church in Laodecia: The church that sits on the fence is called to make a choice and stand for something. They think they are one thing, yet are in reality something else. Again, they are called to repent and are asked to let Jesus in. If they overcome they will sit beside Jesus. Question: will you continue to pay the cost to follow Jesus?

Meditate on each church and determine what the Lord is saying to you specifically. Give thanks that you have an opportunity to be an overcomer.

What is Jesus saying to you?

47. RELATIONSHIPS

Scripture

If your brother or sister sins, go and point out their fault, just between the two of you. If they listen to you, you have won them over. But if they will not listen, take one or two others along, so that 'every matter may be established by the testimony of two or three witnesses.' If they still refuse to listen, tell it to the church; and if they refuse to listen even to the church, treat them as you would a pagan or a tax collector. (Matthew 18:15-17)

The Heart of Jesus for You

Jesus says: Hand over your relationships to me. Those who have hurt you or have caused offence - hand them over to me. It's not that you should ignore any responsibility you have, it's just that the first thing you should do is to come to me about the relationship issue and not to hold on to any anger or hurt. Cast your cares on to me. I will tell you what to do and I will give you the words to say. Do not let the situation fester and turn poisonous. You will have to try and reconcile with the person, but do it in my time and with my words. Again, I tell you not to cherish the hurt or offence, but cast those on me, in order that you can continue to know my freedom in your life. Be brave and let me show you how to reconcile. If the other person does not want to do that, then let them go on their way. You can continue in freedom and peace. Do not hold onto offence, but hand your relationships over to me...

Thought

I can remember when I was younger, I had a good friend. I respected him and he taught me a lot of great things, particularly to do with music. I was playing in a band for a musical we were performing at Poole Arts Centre in southern England. My friend was also involved and it was a wonderful and busy time. Shortly after I got back to London, I received a letter from my friend accusing me of disloyalty and turning my back upon him. I truly did not know where it had all come from. I was hurt - very hurt - by the letter. Our friendship never recovered. I held onto the letter for a long time and if I felt my anger towards him was waning, I would pull out the letter and re-read it and my anger would well up once again. That was until my wife told me to tear up the letter and throw it into the bin. This all happened before I was married, so you can see how long I nurtured the hurt. I had to repent of my actions and attitude and hand over that relationship to the Lord. Ever since then I've tried to keep short accounts with relationships. I don't want anything festering in my heart. Later on, I found out that there were other very unhealthy things going on in my friend's life. So, I lifted him up to the Lord.

Do not cherish or nurture offence in relationships. The apostle Peter writes: 'Do not repay evil with evil or insult with insult. On the contrary, repay evil with blessing, because to this you were called so that you may inherit a blessing.' (1 Peter 3:9)

What is Jesus saying to you?

48. CONTINUE

Scripture

Elisha sent a messenger to say to him, "Go, wash yourself seven times in the Jordan, and your flesh will be restored and you will be cleansed." (2 Kings 5:10)

But Naaman went away angry and said, "I thought that he would surely come out to me and stand and call on the name of the LORD his God, wave his hand over the spot and cure me of my leprosy. (2 Kings 5:11)

Naaman's servants went to him and said, "My father, if the prophet had told you to do some great thing, would you not have done it? How much more, then, when he tells you, 'Wash and be cleansed'!" (2 Kings 5:13)

So he went down and dipped himself in the Jordan seven times, as the man of God had told him, and his flesh was restored and became clean like that of a young boy. (2 Kings 5:14)

The Heart of Jesus for You

Jesus says: Hold on and do not give up. I understand

that it can be tough and that it can look like either I have abandoned you or that I am not able to make what needs to happen happen next. Shall we just laugh at that together? Do you really believe that either of those statements are true? They are not true, but there are reasons as to why things have not quite fallen into place yet. Listen to me. You are not too weak to continue. You're not too tired to finish the race. You do not lack the faith needed to see it through. I am your strength. I am your rest. I am your help. Turn your eyes upon me and fix your gaze fully on me and enjoy who I am. Worship and adore. As you do this the waiting will not seem as long because you are distracted by what you will be doing for all eternity - worshipping...

Thought

In 2 Kings 5 we read the story of Namaan and his healing. He came to Elisha as he had heard he would be able to cure him of leprosy. Elisha heard of the situation and sent a messenger to Namaan, telling him to wash in the Jordan river. Namaan's initial response is in 2 King 5:

11: 'Naman went away angry and said, "I thought that he would surely come out to me and stand and call on the name of the Lord his God, wave his hand over spot and cure me of my leprosy."'

How many times I have said those words as I sought to walk the narrow way by faith:

- I thought God would show me the way by now
- I thought God was going to do it this way
- I thought God's breakthrough would've happened by now
- I thought I would be in a different place by now
- I thought things were going to work out differently
- I thought, I thought, I thought…

We all have a preconception of how we think God would or should work in our journey. Countless times I've thought that breakthrough was coming or that I was going in a certain direction, only for things not to go that way. Initially, Namaan was disappointed and angry at the way things were working out. Pride crept in and he went off in a rage. It was the servants of Namaan who challenged him. The servants said: "My father, if the prophet had told you to do some great thing, would you not have done it? How much more, then, when he tells you, 'Wash and be cleansed'!" (2 Kings 5:13).

Namaan's response to God's way is often our response to God's way. Possibly you have said: "I thought God would work in a spectacular way for me". But maybe the Lord wants to keep you humble and do it His way for His glory.

What is Jesus saying to you?

49. BLESSING

Scripture

The LORD bless you and keep you;

the LORD make his face shine on you

and be gracious to you;

the LORD turn his face toward you

and give you peace. (Numbers 6:24-26)

The Heart of Jesus for You

Jesus says: I bless your spirit to know hope rising rather than despondency flourishing. I bless your spirit to know faith increasing rather than unbelief growing. I bless your spirit to know dreams realised rather than disappointment remaining. I bless your spirit to continue to walk the narrow road rather than trying to make the road wider and easier. I bless your spirit to persevere even when you feel weak. I bless your spirit to know the plans I have for you are to bless you, even if you can't see anything happening at all. I bless your spirit to know that I can bring water from the desert and bring life out of death. I bless you even when you might get frustrated with me because things are not working out the way you thought they might. All you need is my blessing for my blessing is me adding myself to you and I am all you need…

Thought

God wants to bless you. My friend from Iris[11] Global, a mission organisation, called Surprise said to me that God's blessing means that He adds himself to you. When God blesses you it doesn't necessarily mean that you prosper financially (although you could) or in your career (but you might). It means that God is with you and adds himself to you. In that adding you then will prosper in different ways. You prosper only because God is with you.

Joseph experienced the blessing of the Lord in the darkest of times. Look at what Scripture says of Joseph:

The LORD was with Joseph so that he <u>prospered</u>, and he lived in the house of his Egyptian master. (Genesis 39:2)

Joseph found <u>favour</u> in his eyes and became his attendant. Potiphar put him in charge of his household,

---

[11] https://www.irisglobal.org

and he entrusted to his care everything he owned.
(Genesis 39:4)

From the time he put him in charge of his household
and of all that he owned, the LORD blessed the household
of the Egyptian because of Joseph. The blessing of the
LORD was on everything Potiphar had, both in the house
and in the field. (Genesis 39:5)

...the LORD was with him; he showed him kindness
and granted him favour in the eyes of the prison warden.
(Genesis 39:21)

The warden paid no attention to anything under
Joseph's care, because the LORD was with Joseph and gave
him success in whatever he did. (Genesis 39:23)

Joseph responded to all this blessing by saying: "I
cannot do it," Joseph replied to Pharaoh, "but God will
give Pharaoh the answer he desires." (Genesis 41:16).
Joseph gave all the glory to God. He may have started off
in his life slightly arrogant, but he learnt humility on the
journey of faith and gave all the glory to the Lord.

What is Jesus saying to you?

50. STORMS

Scripture

When the storm has swept by, the wicked are gone, but the righteous stand firm forever. (Proverbs 10:25)

You have been a refuge for the poor, a refuge for the needy in their distress, a shelter from the storm and a shade from the heat. (Isaiah 25:4)

The Heart of Jesus for You

Jesus says: In the midst of this storm, with no land in sight, rest in me. I am the life that surrounds you and is keeping you safe. Do not fear that you can see no end to the storm or that you can see no land. You are in the safest place, even though at the moment it can seem dangerous. You can try and swim somewhere, but your progress will be negligible and tiring. Better to rest in me. Float and drift with me. I will never let you go under, even as the waves swell around you and over you. There is a current that you cannot see that is taking you to the places that I want you to go. It is the Holy Spirit current. You can try and go your own way, or surrender yourself to the Holy Spirit current. You may feel that there is no end in sight or no opportunities to be had. That is a lie from the enemy. Hope is at hand…

Thought

On the journey of faith, it can feel that you are in a constant storm. You can feel as though you are being tossed from wave to wave as you seek to do the Lord's will day by day, moment by moment. It can be tiring. I understand that. You feel as though sometimes you just cannot go on. I get that as well. But you can go on and you can be refreshed in the middle of the storm. You just have to focus on Jesus, not on yourself.

Many times we get tired because we swim against the current rather than go with the current. I see a picture of a rough stormy sea and I am looking down on it from above. It looks chaotic and dangerous, with no apparent purpose or direction. Yet, as I look at it a little longer, I can see beneath the surface a current of the Holy Spirit that is forging a way through the storm to the place that God wants you to go.

Jesus said: 'For whoever wants to save their life will lose it, but whoever loses their life for me will find it.' (Matthew 16:25). Don't try and work your way out of the storm. Surrender all to Jesus and let His current lead you to where your Heavenly Father wants you to go.

What is Jesus saying to you?

51. TRAPPED

Scripture

It is for freedom that Christ has set us free. Stand firm, then, and do not let yourselves be burdened again by a yoke of slavery. (Galatians 5:1)

The Heart of Jesus for You

Jesus says: You may feel as though you are trapped in an impossible box at the moment, but I am coming. You may feel that you have no choices and that your hands are tied, but I am coming. You may feel that you cannot see any options from which to choose a path, but I am coming. You may feel that you have no resources on which to live, but I am coming. Hope deferred makes the heart grow sick and you have been waiting for so long now, but I'm coming. In the waiting, your faith has been strengthened and you have walked the narrow path. You have sung songs of worship in times of affliction and difficulty and you have continuously offered prayers to me. Hope is here. I am here. Doors will be opening. Opportunities will be closing in. Rejoice for the next step in the journey of faith is coming. Declare: I shall not fear for you are with me. I am coming…

Thought

I hate the thought of small spaces and getting trapped. Potholing and I will never meet. The idea of being restricted, unable to move, can be a fearful thing, and spiritually many of you may feel trapped with no way out. You may have had prophetic words, you may know the promises of God, you may have been faithful, but it looks like things have come to a dead end and you are trapped. Hear me in this: there is no such thing as a dead end with the Lord and the gospel doesn't bring imprisonment, but freedom. The hope that we have, in such situations as feeling trapped, is that we are in reality not trapped, nor has the Lord forgotten or abandoned us.

Paul and Silas were evangelising and, as a result, they were imprisoned in a cold, dark, damp cell. They were flogged. Not a great situation, but they did not lose hope. Their response was not to complain, but to call upon the

King of Kings in the midst of being trapped in a prison and of feeling the pain from the flogging they had received. They worshipped the Lord in the face of an apparent dead end. Eventually, they were released and what did they do? They went out and continued to evangelise and tell people about Jesus. You may feel that your prison is a dead-end job or a lack of finance, or no job or home. When you are in that place of feeling trapped, I encourage you to be like Paul and Silas:

1. Tell people about Jesus.

2. Worship and pray.

3. In the new situation, when it comes, repeat 1 and 2.

What is Jesus saying to you?

52. PURITY

Scripture

Create in me a pure heart, O God, and renew a steadfast spirit within me. (Psalms 51:10)

Who may ascend the mountain of the LORD? Who may stand in his holy place? The one who has clean hands and a pure heart, who does not trust in an idol or swear by a false god. (Psalm 24:3-4)

The Heart of Jesus for You

Jesus says: Your purity is one of the most important weapons. Lose it and you could get overrun by the enemy. If you open a door you can let anything in. Seek purity and do not give in to the impurity calling you and tempting you to surrender to your lusts and worldly desires. It will say it's okay, but it is not. Call on my name for help in those moments and I will be there. It is easy to fall into a pit of sin and even easier just to decide to stay there for a while. Look up and you will see me waiting for you. Lift up your head and your hands and you will always find hope. Reach up to me and I will pull you out of the pit and I will pull you into hope. Repent, confess, receive my forgiveness and once again walk in the light. Walk in purity. You never need to stay in your sin just because you wonder whether I would forgive you again as you have sinned so many times. I always forgive those who repent. Come back to me and you will find a welcome…

Thought

You don't just fall into purity, you fight for purity. You have to want to be pure. You need to desire to be holy. It doesn't just happen to you. Purity is a battle that we daily fight in the power of the Holy Spirit. We don't fight for purity in our own strength. We will fail. Every time. We need the strength of the Holy Spirit within us to fight the battle for purity and win against temptation.

Impurity is an open door for the enemy to do more damage in your life. Impurity will give the enemy a handhold in your life that could develop into a foothold and then into a stronghold. The only way back from there is true repentance and the resumption of purity.

But the wonderful thing is that God loves it when his children repent. He doesn't stand over us angry or judgemental as we come back to him. No. He is dancing with joy as we come to him and repent. It says in Roman 2:4: 'Or do you show contempt for the riches of his kindness, forbearance and patience, not realising that God's kindness is intended to lead you to repentance?' (Romans 2:4)

What is Jesus saying to you?

53. STRENGTH

Scripture

You gave abundant showers, O God; you refreshed your weary inheritance. (Psalm 68:9)

I love you, LORD, my strength. The LORD is my rock, my fortress and my deliverer; my God is my rock, in whom I take refuge, my shield and the horn of my salvation, my stronghold. (Psalm 18:1-2)

The Heart of Jesus for You

Jesus says: I see your exhaustion and your weariness. I see that you're wondering why you are so tired. You do not need to be doing physical work to get exhausted and weary. Waiting can be so draining. Not knowing what is going to happen next is tiring. Faith can be exhausting and exhilarating. Just know that in your exhaustion I am your strength. I am your strength to continue to wait, to have faith. 'Come to me all you who are weary and burdened and I will give you rest'. (Matthew 11:28) This is a time when, because of tiredness, you can go looking for refreshment in all the wrong places. Those worldly things will tire you out all the more, after giving an illusionary rest. Take the first step and come to me. Call on my name. I will not disappoint. I will give you rest and I will strengthen you to finish this stage of your journey...

Thought

As followers of Jesus we are called to a disciplined alertness. It's all too easy to switch off and be undisciplined in times that are tough on the journey of faith. Jesus calls his followers to be disciplined and alert in the day of trials. If we don't then we will continually get tired and shut down as a way of coping with the situation. Jesus calls us to wake up.

1. He tells us to wake up because we do not know when He's coming back. It would be awful to think that we were spiritually sleeping when Jesus comes back. Since we don't know when that is, we must continually cultivate an attitude of being spiritually awake. 'Therefore, keep watch because you do not know when the owner of the house will come back—whether in the evening, or at midnight, or

when the rooster crows, or at dawn.' (Mark 13:35)

2. We become fully awakened when we stay in the presence of the Lord. His glory awakens the sleepiest soul. It says in Luke 9:32, when Jesus was transfigured: 'Peter and his companions were very sleepy, but when they became fully awake, they saw his glory and the two men standing with him.' (Luke 9:32). The glory of Jesus awoke the sleeping disciples.

3. Jesus tells us to stay awake at all times because the cares of this life can wear your heart down. He tells us to pray at all times, so that you may have strength to continue in every and any situation. 'Be careful, or your hearts will be weighed down with carousing, drunkenness and the anxieties of life, and that day will close on you suddenly like a trap. For it will come on all those who live on the face of the whole Earth. Be always on the watch, and pray that you may be able to escape all that is about to happen, and that you may be able to stand before the Son of Man.' (Luke 21:34-36)

Don't go looking for refreshment and restoration in all the wrong places. Go to Jesus, let his glory awake you, and revitalise you and be ready for His coming back.

What is Jesus saying to you?

54. STRESS

Scripture

The LORD gives strength to his people; the LORD blesses his people with peace. (Psalms 29:11)

You will keep in perfect peace those whose minds are steadfast, because they trust in you. (Isaiah 26:3)

"Because this people has rejected the gently flowing waters of Shiloah and rejoices over Rezin and the son of Remaliah… (Isaiah 8:6)

The Heart of Jesus for You

Jesus says: Stress arises when you try to work out where tomorrow's bread will come from. Stress arises when you lean on your own understanding. Stress arises when you try to work it all out by yourself and try to build your own future, rather than letting me build your future. Do not look at what others have, as jealousy and offence will rise up and tie you up in unholy knots. Look at me. I will say it again: look at me. Focus your gaze on me and trust me for your daily strength and for your needs, even when you're old and grey. A life lived in dependence on me will truly bring me glory. And it can be stress free, as you don't have to worry about anything. Haven't you lost the right to worry because you've experienced my constant faithfulness? Worship and give thanks. I seek those disciples who will daily surrender and live a life of complete submission to me...

Thought

The journey of faith can induce stress, if we let it. Faith demands uncertainty and we as people love certainty. Certainty that we have enough money in the bank. Certainty that we have somewhere to live. Certainty that we will always know the next step. But, for the follower of Jesus, certainty is not helpful, particularly if you want your faith to grow.

Mark 14:43-52 tells us of one of the disciples who fled naked after Jesus was arrested. It is a bleak scene, desolate, with no sign of the courageous words, such as 'I will never leave you.' Jesus is abandoned and left alone. Desperate situations have a way of stripping us of our facades and revealing who we truly are and what we would do. We may say, "Oh, I would never have left Jesus." Really?

In times that are stressful and we want to run away and it feels like everything is out of control, we need to re-imagine ourselves as dancers. Spiritual dancers spinning around. To stop themselves from getting dizzy, dancers fix their gaze in one spot. As things seem to spiral out of control make sure you fix your gaze on the one spot: JESUS.

What is Jesus saying to you?

55. DOODLEBUGS

Scripture

The weapons we fight with are not the weapons of the world. On the contrary, they have divine power to demolish strongholds. (2 Corinthians 10:4)

Fight the good fight of the faith. Take hold of the eternal life to which you were called when you made your good confession in the presence of many witnesses. (1 Timothy 6:12)

I have fought the good fight, I have finished the race, I have kept the faith. (2 Timothy 4:7)

The Heart of Jesus for You

Jesus says: Do not bow down on the day of spiritual attack. Satan's attacks can be like unspiritual dirty bombs, continually flying into life. His aim is to destroy and discourage, to stop the work and purpose of God in your life. In World War 2, London was bombarded with 'doodlebugs', flying bombs that made a loud noise and randomly dropped to the ground when they ran out of fuel. The people heard the bombs and watched to see where they would land. Satan's doodlebugs are all around you, but none shall land on you. They may come close and you may feel some of the effects from them, but you shall be protected. You're surrounded by angels. You're surrounded by me. In the midst of the flying bombs of Satan, do not crumple or bow down in fear. Lift up your heads and worship me when all seems lost, for I am with you and my purpose in your life will prevail. Stand firm. Stand firm. Stand firm…

Thought

When the spiritual attacks of Satan are increasing and show no signs of coming to an end, our reaction can be to buckle and give up. I get it. It seems like what is happening - the attacks, the unclarity, the lack of peace - it's just too long and difficult. With the Psalmist we cry out, 'How long, O Lord, how long?' (Psalm 6:3)

I wish I could tell you "not much longer", but I can't say that. What I can say is to stand firm and don't give up. You are a soldier of Christ. You are a warrior in battle. The battle is for God's glory - not that His glory is ever in doubt - and we want to crush anything the rebels against the Lord. It's not about us. It is about Him. The battle is fierce. Cowards do not stand in the heat of battle. You are not a coward.

In the battle there is no better shelter than the presence of God. It is the safest place to be. There is a strengthening that occurs as we get into the presence of God, that enables us to continue to stand in the battle. We give up too easily sometimes. Don't. Just stand. In the presence of God. In prayer. As the doodlebugs of Satan crash all around you, just stand and you will see victory.

What is Jesus saying to you?

56. SHORT

Scripture

So then, just as you received Christ Jesus as Lord, continue to live your lives in him, rooted and built up in him, strengthened in the faith as you were taught, and overflowing with thankfulness. (Colossians 2:6-7)

… and in Christ you have been brought to fullness. (Colossians 2:10)

The Heart of Jesus for You

Jesus says: Don't stop short of all that I have planned for you. I realise that the journey has been difficult and tough, but I have been building within you a resilient faith, a faith that will cut through future difficult situations, a faith that will not buckle. You may be tired and exhausted emotionally, spiritually and physically. You may not know what the future holds. Do not give up now. Keep on going with a tenacity that refuses to let go. You are close to the shore that will lead you to the next stage. The journey of faith is not just one step of faith and you are all done. The journey of faith is many steps of faith and at each step I am preparing you for the next. The next stage is wonderful. Do not let your faith get depleted. Speak to yourself and awaken the gift of faith that I have placed within you. Do not stop short...

Thought

There is a story in the Old Testament that makes me sad. Numbers 32 tells the story of the Reubenites and Gadites, two of the tribes of Israel who wandered the desert for forty years. It says in Numbers 32: 'The Reubenites and Gadites, who had very large herds and flocks, **saw** that the lands of Jazer and Gilead were suitable for livestock.' (Numbers 32:1). The story continues: 'If we have found favour in your eyes,' they said, 'let this land be given to your servants as our possession. Do not make us cross the Jordan.' (Numbers 32:5)

'Do not make us cross the Jordan'! They have just spent forty years getting there. They had seen water from a rock, bread from Heaven and had shoes that never wore out. They had heard of the parting of the Red Sea from the previous generation and had looked forward to the Promised Land. Yet, at the last moment, they were diverted from God's destiny because of what they saw with their eyes. That's an issue. When things have gone on for a long time and the journey of faith has been tough, we can start to look at things with our worldly eyes rather than with the eyes of faith. The world starts to tempt us and, like the Reubenites and Gadites, we are enticed to stop our journey of faith and fall short of God's destiny for us. We settle for less than the Lord has for us. Don't stop short. Keep on going, You WILL finish this journey of faith and God will be glorified in your life!

What is Jesus saying to you?

57. TURNAROUND

Scripture

And we know that in all things God works for the good of those who love him, who have been called according to his purpose. (Romans 8:28)

Our God, will you not judge them? For we have no power to face this vast army that is attacking us. We do not know what to do, but our eyes are on you. (2 Chronicles 20:12)

The Heart of Jesus for You

Jesus says: Every situation, good or bad, I can turn around for my glory and for people's salvation and for your good. I am the turnaround Saviour. I can take the deepest, darkest and most dysfunctional situations and transform them into something glorious. I can take the person who seems the least likely to follow me, the most hopeless or rebellious person and redeem them. No person and no situation is too remote. There is not a hopeless person or situation that I cannot save. The turnaround may not look like how you would do it and it may not be in your timing, but the partners of hope are patience and trust. Trust in me and do not rely on yourself. Patiently waiting on hope means not trying to manufacture an outcome. Patiently waiting on hope is waiting with your eyes lifted towards Heaven, acknowledging that you don't know what to do and that in the midst of waiting for the turnaround to happen, you will make a decision to worship Father, Son and Holy Spirit...

Thought

We all face situations which we want the Lord to turn completely around. We have children or brothers and sisters who are far from the Lord and we long for them to follow Jesus. We have financial situations and illness problems that seem insurmountable. There can be so many issues that have the potential to crush us. BUT GOD. Your God is the God who turns things around and specialises in impossible situations!

Here's a little poem I wrote to encourage you:

I've lain in the dust and you've revived me by your

word

I've descended into darkness and you've shone your light.

You are the God who turns situations around

First shall be last and the last shall be first

The humble lifted up

And the poor shall be made rich

You heal and you restore

Through Jesus Christ my lord

You are the turnaround God

There are times when I have ignored you and gone and done my own thing

But every time you're running towards me with a robe and a ring

In every situation there is a diamond in the rough

In every situation you are more than enough[12].

What is Jesus saying to you?

---

[12] ©Alan Kilpatrick, 2020

58. PRESSED

Scripture

But we have this treasure in jars of clay to show that this all-surpassing power is from God and not from us. We are hard pressed on every side, but not crushed; perplexed, but not in despair; persecuted, but not abandoned; struck down, but not destroyed. We always carry around in our body the death of Jesus, so that the life of Jesus may also be revealed in our body. For we who are alive are always being given over to death for Jesus' sake, so that his life may also be revealed in our mortal body. So then, death is at work in us, but life is at work in you. (2 Corinthians 4:7-12)

The Heart of Jesus for You

Jesus says: You may be hard pressed on every side, feeling that the walls are closing in and that there is no end to the unrelenting pressure. However, with my presence with you, you will not be crushed. You may feel confused and perplexed by what is happening, disappointed with the way things seem to be turning out, but if my presence is with you, you will not despair nor lose hope. You may feel that the attacks will never stop and that the battle seems to be increasing rather than decreasing, but with me by your side you're not alone, isolated or abandoned. You may feel that you have been struck down, that the news you've just received was like a boxer punching you in the stomach and you have fallen onto the ground, but with me by your side you will not be destroyed. You may feel fragile and broken, but my light and life is within you, shining through the cracks in your life. You are weak, but I am strong and I am for you and I choose you. You're on my team. The way you live for me in terms of difficulty will be a revelation of me to those who do not yet know me...

Thought

I have to confess that there have been times on my journey of faith that I have felt that I've been in a boxing ring with an expert boxer and sometimes they've landed a punch that has knocked me to the ground. Maybe it was news I received. Or maybe, it was a lack of breakthrough that finally got on top of me.

Even though I was knocked to the ground, I was not out. Even though I felt fragile, I was not broken. Even though I felt overwhelmed, I did not drown. Not because of any strength or giftings I had, but because of Jesus. Only Jesus.

Paul knew what it was to face a daily and constant battle of faith. He was left for dead. He was beaten, imprisoned and vilified. He was misrepresented and slandered. I love the honesty he portrays in 2 Corinthians: 'Indeed, we felt we had received the sentence of death. But this happened that we might not rely on ourselves but on God, who raises the dead. He has delivered us from such a deadly peril, and he will deliver us again. On him we have set our hope that he will continue to deliver us, as you help us by your prayers. Then many will give thanks on our behalf for the gracious favour granted us in answer to the prayers of many.' (2 Corinthians 1:9-11)

Take these times as a praise opportunity. Rejoice that you can't do it and that you feel helpless and overwhelmed, as this shows that only God can do it. And he will do it. Not for your glory. But for His!

What is Jesus saying to you?

59. SEATED

Scripture

When I tried to understand all this, it troubled me deeply till I entered the sanctuary of God; then I understood their final destiny. (Psalm 73:16-17)

And God raised us up with Christ and seated us with him in the Heavenly realms in Christ Jesus…(Ephesians 2:6)

The Heart of Jesus for You

Jesus says: Come and sit back up on your seat in the Heavenly places and get a Heavenly perspective once again on your situation. Perspective is everything. I know that your situation is difficult and that you are perplexed. Despair may be starting to set in and maybe you have begun to lean on your own understanding rather than trusting in me with your whole heart. Do you want to wallow in despair or do you want to have a different perspective on all that is happening at the moment? I understand the pain and despair. You have not suffered more than I have. Make a choice to rise above all of the conflict, affliction and warfare and sit a while with me. Let us look down on what is happening. Let's talk about it. Let your heart be changed by my presence. Choose to sit in the Heavenly places with me and get a Heavenly perspective today…

Thought

Psalm 73 is a powerful psalm that teaches us all about the necessity of getting a Heavenly perspective on the journey of faith. The writer, Asaph, tells of his struggle with envying the arrogant and the prosperity of the wicked. Why are those who do evil prosperous? Why do they not get ill or have the struggles that we have? Why can they do as they want without repercussions? It is a recognisable struggle that we all may face as we try to work out what is happening in today's world or even on a road journey of faith. Why has that follower of Jesus been blessed more than me? Much more!

The writer's story gets more intense as he declares that he has remained pure and has obeyed God, yet he is afflicted every day. Then we read in verse 17: 'till I entered the sanctuary of God; then I understood the final destiny.' The Passion Translation translates that verse like this: 'But then one day I was brought into the sanctuaries of God, and in the light of glory, my distorted perspective vanished. Then I understood that the destiny of the wicked was near!' (Psalm 73:17, TPT) The Message says: 'Until I entered the sanctuary of God. Then I saw the whole picture.' (Psalm 73:17, MSG)

The encouragement of Jesus to you today is not to focus on the apparent success of those doing evil or the greater prosperity of your brother and sister. If you do, your heart will become hard. As soon as you feel the envy creeping in then get into the presence of the Lord, worship Him and let your perspective be transformed in the light of His glory, for a heavenly perspective is everything.

What is Jesus saying to you...

60. UNCERTAINTY

Scripture

The LORD is exalted, for he dwells on high; he will fill Zion with his justice and righteousness. He will be the sure foundation for your times, a rich store of salvation and wisdom and knowledge; the fear of the LORD is the key to this treasure. (Isaiah 33:5-6)

Neither do we go beyond our limits by boasting of work done by others. Our hope is that, as your faith continues to grow, our sphere of activity among you will greatly expand… (2 Corinthians 10:15)

The Heart of Jesus for You

Jesus says: Do not be anxious in the times of uncertainty. Uncertainty is the mould in which faith is formed and shaped. Without uncertainty, faith cannot develop and grow. That is why you can rejoice in all circumstances. My Father is developing your faith in difficult times. My grace will flow to you in those times if you trust in me and surrender to the workings of my

Father in your life. When you take things into your own hands, then they can start to fall apart. I redeem situations. I bring life out of death. Nothing is uncertain to me, so look to me and hold onto me, as I navigate you through uncertain times and as your faith is strengthened and developed...

Thought

I have said this before in previous chapters, but I will say it again: UNCERTAINTY GROWS FAITH. In fact, I will go even further and say that faith only grows in the soil of uncertainty or impossibility. The church needs to wake up to the reality that full bank accounts and multiple programmes do not show great faith. Great faith is shown by walking into the realm of uncertainty and impossibility with no chance of success unless God intervenes.

I suspect as you read this that you are going through one of the most challenging seasons that you have faced. Don't give up, but once again: 'Trust in the Lord completely, and do not rely on your own opinions. With all your heart, rely on him to guide you, and he will lead you in every decision you make. Become intimate with him in whatever you do and he will lead you wherever you go' (Proverbs 3:5-6, TPT)

In our uncertainty we press into the certainty of the Lord. He is preparing a way for you, even if you can't see it. AW Tozer[13] writes: 'We must meet the uncertainties of this world with the certainty of the world to come.' Oswald Chambers[14] writes: 'Certainty is the mark of the common sense life - gracious uncertainty is the mark of the spiritual life.' Wait on the Lord in the midst of uncertainty. He is able.

What is Jesus saying to you?

---

[13] https://www.christianquotes.info/images/a-w-tozer-quote-uncertainties

[14] https://calming-quotes.blogspot.com/2021/03/christian-quotes-about-uncertainty.html

61. MISSIONARY

Scripture

I, even I, have spoken; yes, I have called him. I will bring him, and he will succeed in his mission. (Isaiah 48:15)

Then I heard the voice of the Lord saying, "Whom shall I send? And who will go for us?" And I said, "Here am I. Send me! (Isaiah 6:8)

The Heart of Jesus for You

Jesus says: You are a missionary wherever you live and whatever you do. You are a missionary. I've sent you to the people you're with, people that I love dearly, even though they do not yet follow me. You are the channel I want to use to tell them of my love for them. Do not be afraid. I will give you the words to say, but do not miss the opportunity to share the good news. Not everyone will receive it and some may think that you are crazy. However, some will receive the seeds you scatter and a harvest will follow. You may feel ill-equipped or foolish or that you lack the necessary training. That is OK. It means you don't want to rely on your own intellect, but that you have to rely on me. I break off negative words that have been spoken over you saying that you cannot do this or you cannot do that, or that you will never amount to anything. I declare the truth that I have chosen you and you are my missionary...

Thought

I remember when I was very young hearing the phrase that people were going to the mission field. I pictured people going to stand in a field. I thought it was strange. Later on, I realised my misconception.

For me, growing up in Scotland, missionaries were people going abroad to tell people about Jesus. Then my parents became 'missionaries' in Scotland. A change in paradigm.

You could be a missionary at home. You are a missionary. A missionary is a person on a mission. Jesus has commissioned you on a mission to tell people about the good news. You don't have to go abroad.

Isaiah 6 is often used as a chapter about missionaries.

"Whom should I send?" we hear God call. "Here am I. Send me", replies Isaiah. There is nothing in there about whom shall I send **abroad**. It is simply "Who is prepared to go and tell others about me?" Isaiah's reply, I'm sure, was one of excitement and enthusiasm, not one of hiding and hoping that God didn't spot him. You even have a sending organisation on your mission: the Trinity. On you go, and tell others about Jesus.

What is Jesus saying to you?

62. OVERTHINKING

Scripture

Seek the LORD while he may be found; call on him while he is near. Let the wicked forsake their ways and the unrighteous their thoughts. Let them turn to the LORD, and he will have mercy on them, and to our God, for he will freely pardon. "For my thoughts are not your thoughts, neither are your ways my ways," declares the LORD. "As the Heavens are higher than the Earth, so are my ways higher than your ways and my thoughts than your thoughts. As the rain and the snow come down from Heaven, and do not return to it without watering the Earth and making it bud and flourish, so that it yields seed for the sower and bread for the eater, so is my word that goes out from my mouth: It will not return to me empty, but will accomplish what I desire and achieve the purpose for which I sent it. (Isaiah 55:6-11)

The Heart of Jesus for You

Jesus says: Overthinking is not a gift of the Spirit.

There are some situations that you will not be able to work out and you should not even try to work them out. Overthinking is doubt in disguise and continually overthinking leads to unbelief. Sometimes you may have seen my breakthrough or provision and you are grateful. Then you have started to overthink or walk in doubt about future things as though I have run out of ideas, possibilities, power or finances. I have not! What I have done I can do again, in the same way or in a completely different way. The journey I have called you on is not just one step and it's all done. It's a lot of steps and each step is different and requires faith. Some steps are easy and some steps require more faith. I am with you at every step. Do not overthink the journey and do not lean on your own understanding. Let every step you take be a step of faith. Do not think or worry about the future steps you will take or worry about the provision or strategies for these. I will give you enough faith and strategy for the next step...

Thought

I reckon that I could get a PhD in 'overthinking'. If I

want to buy something I research to the utmost degree, to the point that I can't actually make a decision. Overthinking immobilises you. You can know everything about a situation, but that can lead you into immobility. Knowledge doesn't make the faith walk any easier. Only Jesus does that.

Faith doesn't demand overthinking, but demands surrender and submission to Jesus. The journey of faith is not one step and it's all over. In Numbers 33 we read about the stages of Israel's journey in the wilderness. In forty years they moved forty one times. Millions of people moved regularly through a desert, not knowing when their journey would be over, led supernaturally by a cloud and pillar of fire. I am sure many times they would sit by a campfire overthinking what was happening. How long would this journey be? Has God forgotten them? Is the next move the last move?

You just have to trust the Lord and not lean on your own understanding. That is what overthinking is: leaning on your own understanding. So, trust in the Lord with every fibre of your being.

What is Jesus saying to you?

63. WAIT

Scripture

In the morning, LORD, you hear my voice; in the morning I lay my requests before you and wait expectantly. (Psalm 5:3)

Wait for the LORD; be strong and take heart and wait for the LORD. (Psalm 27:14)

We wait in hope for the LORD; he is our help and our shield. (Psalm 33:20)

The Heart of Jesus for You

Jesus says: Faith and uncertainty are two sides of the same coin. You may feel uncertain about something - good! Let your faith step in and grow. Some of you will feel you have great faith, but are confused about what will happen next. This means you will have to continue to look to your Father in Heaven and fix your eyes on Him. Uncertainty and confusion are not necessarily signs that you are on the wrong path. It is just that you don't need all of the information yet or that there is a spiritual battle going on. In both cases: pray and worship. Stand and look at me. Wait patiently in the corridor until the right door opens. Journeying with me is like walking with a blurred photograph, where you can't see all of the details and may only start to come into focus when my timing is right or the battle has finished. Confusion turns to clarity and then it may start again with the next stage of the journey...

Thought

I believe that doubt and uncertainty are different things. Doubt's basis is fear. Doubts arise out of a fear of something, whereas uncertainty is not knowing which option is right. You know that one of them is probably right, but you're not sure which one.

Doubt in God means that you doubt His ability to do what He promised to do. Uncertainty reflects the fact that you're not sure how He will do it, but you know that He will do it as He is able.

One of the verses in scripture that has been an anchor for me is Psalm 143:8: "Let morning bring the word of your unfailing love, for I have put my trust in you. Show me the way I should go, for to you I entrust my life." Waiting on the Lord is coming to Him day by day, in the midst of uncertainty, and declaring the truths found in Psalm 143:8.

Truth 1. I know that God is going to speak about my situation.

Truth 2. I know that I am loved.

Truth 3. I have faith that He will show me the way.

Truth 4. I surrender all to Him.

What is Jesus saying to you?

64. UN-NORMALISE

Scripture

May God himself, the God of peace, sanctify you through and through. May your whole spirit, soul and body be kept blameless at the coming of our Lord Jesus Christ. (1 Thessalonians 5:23)

So we fix our eyes not on what is seen, but on what is unseen, since what is seen is temporary, but what is unseen is eternal. (2 Corinthians 4:18)

Remember, therefore, what you have received and heard; hold it fast, and repent. But if you do not wake up, I will come like a thief, and you will not know at what time I will come to you. (Revelation 3:3)

"The time has come," he said. "The kingdom of God has come near. Repent and believe the good news!" (Mark 1:15)

The Heart of Jesus for You

Jesus says: Do not normalise sin in your life. Do not say that the sin is okay, as it is only small and it brings me a little comfort and I need some comfort at the moment. There are no acceptable sins in the walk of a disciple. The goal is purity, not compromise. One day you will look back on your life on Earth from the perspective of Heaven and wonder why you were so easily satisfied with the trash that the world could provide, when the rich feast of Heaven was available to you. Earthly things are brambles and trinkets compared to the treasure of knowing me. Start today to walk in purity. Put to death sin in your life and repent and receive my forgiveness. It is never too late! Do you want comfort? Come to me. I am your greatest comfort. Do you love sinning more than you love me? I am your only hope. Godliness is so important to pursue in the power of the Holy Spirit. It is of the greatest value on Earth and prepares you for eternity. Do not normalise sin…

Thought

As sin bombards you with temptation, it can become attractive to justify and normalise your sin habits. Please hear me that I'm not talking from theory, but my own experience. We sin because it is either pleasurable or it is a comfort to us. Normally, we continually succumb to sin because our body, and our physical needs, are leading our spirit and soul (our emotions and thoughts). That is one reason why people get addicted - their bodies are leading the way that they live and the choices that they make. Again, I know that from experience.

Three things will help us in this battle:

1. Let the Holy Spirit in your spirit lead your body and soul. Let the Holy Spirit grow within your spirit and tell your body and soul to take a back seat as the Spirit of God within you is now in the driving seat. (1 Thessalonians 5:23)

2. The things of this earth will fade away and perish. The things of Heaven will never fade away. This earth is not Heaven. There will be a new Heaven and a new Earth. (2 Cor 4:18)

3. Repent and come back to the Lord. If you have sinned, don't keep away from the Lord, but come back to Him with all humility and repentance. He will forgive and restore, for that is what happens in the gospel. (Rev 3:3, Mark 1:15)

What is Jesus saying to you?

65. ADVENTURE

Scripture

And I tell you that you are Peter, and on this rock I will build my church, and the gates of Hades will not overcome it. (Matthew 16:18)

Shadrach, Meshach and Abednego replied to him, "King Nebuchadnezzar, we do not need to defend ourselves before you in this matter. If we are thrown into the blazing furnace, the God we serve is able to deliver us from it, and he will deliver us from Your Majesty's hand. But even if he does not, we want you to know, Your Majesty, that we will not serve your gods or worship the image of gold you have set up. (Daniel 3:16-18)

They saw that the fire had not harmed their bodies, nor was a hair of their heads singed; their robes were not scorched, and there was no smell of fire on them. (Daniel 3:27)

The Heart of Jesus for You

Jesus says: Don't be surprised when safety is desired

more than risk, faith and adventure, by those in the kingdom of God. You're called to be a risk taker, not to play it safe. You are called to be an adventurer and an explorer in the kingdom and not to sit in the same place, looking at the same things and going through the same motions. You are a pioneer that cuts paths through areas that have not been explored. When you tell people about your adventures, they may look at you as though you are silly and careless. Don't accept that. You are the Indiana Jones in the Kingdom of God. Do not be risk-averse as faith will die. Come on, let's go on an adventure together...

Thought

I once talked to a leader in a denomination where I applied for a job to lead a church. I didn't get an interview and I asked the leader why. I wanted to find out, so I could learn. He said the main reasons for not getting an interview were:

1. I had been a missionary for the past four years.

2. I was too risky and the church is risk-averse.

On another occasion, when I asked again why I didn't

get an interview and I was told that I was 'too adventurous.'

What has happened to the church of Jesus Christ that it has become risk-averse! There's only one response to that and it is repentance. The church needs to repent of its fear of risk and adventure. It needs to lay down the security of safety and pick up the attitude of adventure. Was the church in Acts risk-averse?

AW Tozer[15] said: 'A scared world needs a fearless church.' Jesus said that he would build the church and the gates of Hell would not prevail or stand up against it. (Matthew 16:18) Let me be direct. If a church is risk-averse, then it is not a church built by Jesus. In that case, the gates of Hell have overcome it. However, if Jesus has built the church then it will not be risk-averse and it will overcome Hades, and through that church Jesus will destroy Satan. On our journey of faith we don't need nice well-organised churches. We need fearless churches, willing to take risks for the glory of God.

----

[15] https://quotefancy.com/quote/1446733/Aiden-Wilson-Tozer-A-scared-world-needs-a-fearless-church

Shadrach, Meshach and Abednego (Daniel 3) were not risk-averse. They were fearless and trusted in the Lord no matter the outcome for them. They lived well, had good titles in the King's court, yet there came a point where they had to make a choice. They could kneel in front of the King's idol. Or they could be thrown into a furnace. They would not bow and so they were thrown into the furnace. They survived and their clothes didn't even smell of fire. We serve the same God today!

What is Jesus saying to you?

66. RIGHT

Scripture

"Therefore I tell you, do not worry about your life, what you will eat or drink; or about your body, what you will wear. Is not life more than food, and the body more than clothes? Look at the birds of the air; they do not sow or reap or store away in barns, and yet your Heavenly Father feeds them. Are you not much more valuable than they? Can any one of you by worrying add a single hour to your life? And why do you worry about clothes? See how the flowers of the field grow. They do not labour or spin. Yet I tell you that not even Solomon in all his splendour was dressed like one of these. If that is how God clothes the grass of the field, which is here today and tomorrow is thrown into the fire, will he not much more clothe you— you of little faith? So do not worry, saying, 'What shall we eat?' or 'What shall we drink?' or 'What shall we wear?' For the pagans run after all these things, and your Heavenly Father knows that you need them. But seek first his kingdom and his righteousness, and all these things will be given to you as well. Therefore do not worry about tomorrow, for tomorrow will worry about itself. Each day has enough trouble of its own. (Matthew 6:25-34)

The Heart of Jesus for You

Jesus says: You have lost the right to worry because I have always been faithful to you. When have I ever reneged on any of my promises? Have I not provided for you? Have I abandoned you or been capricious in my dealings with you? Have I neglected you?

It may sometimes feel that I have, but that was part of the process of bringing you to rely on me more. I will not be less than my word. I have been liberal with all my promises and I will not go back on any of them. Trust me. Believe in me.

Let faith awaken and rise up within you. You don't need to keep asking for breakthrough. Breakthrough will come. When you keep asking you are not present to what is happening. Be willing to learn the lesson I have for you in the season you are in. Do not fear for the future, for I do not run out of money, imagination or power. Lay down worry and pick up faith…

Thought

I once put up a Facebook post saying that we have lost the right to worry as we have known and experienced the faithfulness of God. To my surprise not everyone liked it or agreed with me. I'm not looking for everyone to agree with me, I was just surprised that followers of Jesus thought they did have a right to worry. My question to them is why? Why on Earth do you think you have a right to worry, when we serve the King of Kings and Lord of Lords? Worry and concern are two different things. Worry is fear based and irrational. Concern is an attitude that comes out of love and a desire to help if possible. Just to remind you how unbiblical worry is:

- But when they arrest you, do not worry about what to say or how to say it. At that time you will be given what to say…' (Matthew 10:19)
- But make up your mind not to worry beforehand how you will defend yourselves. (Luke 21:14)
- Do not be anxious about anything, but in every

situation, by prayer and petition, with thanksgiving, present your requests to God. (Philippians 4:6)

What is Jesus saying to you?

67. JOY

Scripture

Nehemiah said, "Go and enjoy choice food and sweet drinks, and send some to those who have nothing prepared. This day is holy to our Lord. Do not grieve, for the joy of the LORD is your strength." (Nehemiah 8:10)

Rejoice in the Lord always. I will say it again: Rejoice! (Philippians 4:4)

Though the fig tree does not bud and there are no grapes on the vines, though the olive crop fails and the fields produce no food, though there are no sheep in the pen and no cattle in the stalls, yet I will rejoice in the LORD, I will be joyful in God my Saviour (Habakkuk 3:17-18)

The Heart of Jesus for You

Jesus says: Aim to have joy in all circumstances. It is futile to wait until all the situations in your life are going well until you have joy. Even if that does happen, it will probably be for a fleeting moment. Better to be joyful in all circumstances than to wait for circumstances in which it is easy to be joyful. If you are joyful in difficult circumstances, it reveals that your hope is in me, not in the world and that your joy is in me, not in what happens around you. Let my joy in you overflow into your heart and let my joy in you be the strength you need to thrive through difficult seasons. The Devil hates it when you are joyful in tough circumstances. He hates it, because it is a witness to all around of my hope, and others will want to know why you have joy and hope in such times. Refuse to let go of joy and let me be your strength…

Thought

Joy is not dependent on your current situation. It is dependent on the fulness of the Holy Spirit in your life. If you want more joy, ask to be filled with more of the Holy Spirit, as joy is part of the fruit that will grow within you.

Joy also comes from getting into God's presence (Psalm 16:11). Read your bibles and worship the Lord during a quiet time every day.

We are to be joyful in difficult situations (James 1:2)

This is probably the hardest thing to do.

My encouragement is Paul and Silas singing in prison. Our example is also Jesus (Hebrews 12:2). I'll be honest. I'm not constantly joyful. I wish I was, but I don't have to stay in despair.

Here are some suggestions to encourage joy in your life:

1. Ask the Holy Spirit to fill you.

2. Continue to worship daily in a quiet time.

3. Make a decision to be joyful and act joyfully.

4. Laugh more.

5. Connect with others - in person.

6. Hand all your anxious thoughts to the Lord.

What is Jesus saying to you?

68. DISAPPOINTMENT

Scripture

Do not be anxious about anything, but in every situation, by prayer and petition, with thanksgiving, present your requests to God. (Philippians 4:6)

Jesus gave them this answer: "Truly I tell you, the Son can do nothing by himself; he can do only what he sees his Father doing, because whatever the Father does the Son also does. (John 5:19)

The Heart of Jesus for You

Jesus says: Do you not detach from me because of disappointment. You may not have heard the word you wanted to hear or receive the response you wanted to get, but do not get angry and turn to worldly things to bring you comfort for a brief moment. Draw close to me and I will draw close to you. Press forward and continue to seek me with all your being, even in the midst of disappointment and frustration. For I am working out my plan. You are part of that plan, but maybe you are realising that the way it is working out is different from what you thought. Your worth is not in what you do and your validation is not in the works of people. My words to you validate you and I declare the truth that you are a son or a daughter of God, a warrior of the King of Kings and you have a great value in my eyes…

Thought

In this journey of faith that Jan and I have been on, I have had to work through disappointment again and again. Over a period of time I applied for more than 25 jobs and only got one interview, and then the interview was cancelled. On a few occasions, I talked to the people who had gone through my application to try and find out why I had not been offered an interview. I was regularly told that there were stronger candidates than me. I felt rejected and it hurt. But my worth is not in a job. We have to get to the point where Jesus is enough. It doesn't matter what jobs we have or don't have. It matters that we only do what he wants us to do.

We can have peace in the midst of confusion,

uncertainty and disappointment. It is a gift from the Lord that guards our hearts like a soldier. If we go to Him and present our anxieties and prayers, He will give you peace. He promises that in Scripture.

Stop wallowing in self pity and make a decision to wallow in the presence of the Lord, with prayers and adoration. He has got you and He's got your situation!

What is Jesus saying to you?

69. HIDDEN

Scripture

For you died, and your life is now hidden with Christ in God. (Colossians 3:3)

There is a time for everything,

and a season for every activity under the Heavens:

a time to be born and a time to die,

a time to plant and a time to uproot,

a time to kill and a time to heal,

a time to tear down and a time to build,

a time to weep and a time to laugh,

a time to mourn and a time to dance,

a time to scatter stones and a time to gather them,

a time to embrace and a time to refrain from embracing,

a time to search and a time to give up,

a time to keep and a time to throw away,

a time to tear and a time to mend,

a time to be silent and a time to speak,

a time to love and a time to hate,

a time for war and a time for peace. (Ecclesiastes 3:1-8)

The Heart of Jesus for You

Jesus says: I have had you in a hidden season. You have not been forgotten or abandoned. There is a time for public ministry and there are times of hiddenness. In these times of hiddenness I bring healing, rest, I increase faith as you wait, I gather and I rebuild. I plant spiritual seeds and let the seedlings emerge in the greenhouse of hiddenness. I detox and bring health to your bones. Do not rush to leave the hidden season, even though you feel that you are ready to go. Your times are in my hands. Remain and patiently wait. I am the gardener, tilling up the soil of your heart. All of my children focus on results, but yet do not like the process that needs to happen to get those results. Hiddenness will not last a lifetime, just a season. Do not be in a hurry to get out of this time. Let me form you, reform you, transform you…

Thought

Sometimes it can seem that the Lord has forgotten you. We can feel like King David when he said: I am forgotten as though I were dead; I have become like broken pottery.

235

(Psalms 31:12). However, as far as I can work out, the only thing that the Lord forgets is your sin. He doesn't forget you. We are the ones who tend to forget what the Lord has done for us and when we enter into a hidden season, we complain that He has done nothing for us.

One of the most helpful passages in Scripture about hiddenness is from the story of Elijah. First of all, he tells the King that there will be no rain and there was no rain. He gave an incredible prophetic word. You would think a public ministry beckons, but then the Lord says: "Then the word of the Lord came to Elijah: Leave here, turn eastward and hide in the Kerith Ravine, east of the Jordan. You will drink from the brook, and I have directed the ravens to supply you with food there."1 Kings 17:2-4. Elijah was powerfully used by the Lord and then the Lord told him to go and hide himself.

Afterwards, Elijah was used again powerfully by the Lord. People had seen the supernatural power of God trounce the idols of the day. In addition to that he told King Ahab that it would not rain and it didn't. Now he tells the King to hurry up and get back home as the rain is coming. An incredible ministry encounter and then Elijah runs away afraid.

In both times of hiddenness - one directed by the Lord and one initiated by fear - God provided and ministered to him.

Being used by God can be exhausting. We are weaker than we think, unless we allow the Lord to hide us away for a season, in order that we are refreshed and restored by Him. Do not despise the seasons of hiddenness.

What is Jesus saying to you?

70. ILL-EQUIPPED

Scripture

But the Lord said to Samuel, "Do not consider his appearance or his height, for I have rejected him. The LORD does not look at the things people look at. People look at the outward appearance, but the LORD looks at the heart." (1 Samuel 16:7)

There are different kinds of gifts, but the same Spirit distributes them. There are different kinds of service, but the same Lord. There are different kinds of working, but in all of them and in everyone it is the same God at work. (1 Corinthians 12:4-6)

But David said to Saul, "Your servant has been keeping his father's sheep. When a lion or a bear came and carried off a sheep from the flock, I went after it, struck it and rescued the sheep from its mouth. When it turned on me, I seized it by its hair, struck it and killed it. Your servant has killed both the lion and the bear; this uncircumcised Philistine will be like one of them, because he has defied the armies of the living God. The LORD who rescued me from the paw of the lion and the paw of the bear will rescue me from the hand of this Philistine." (1 Samuel 17:34-37)

The Heart of Jesus for You

Jesus says: You are not ill-equipped or lacking in the necessary skills or gifts for the ministry that I have called you to do. If I call, then I equip and resource. Do not be intimidated by others, who seem to be particularly gifted or strong. Their calling and your calling are different. You are part of the same body, but you are different parts of the body. I look at the heart and the desires of the heart. Do not let jealousy of others' gifting distract you from the path you are on. Rejoice that they can do what they do and get on with what I have called you to do and have gifted you to do. You will be ill-equipped if you try to copy someone else's ministry. Let me continue to equip you for what I have called you to do and do not be intimidated by others...

Thought

I understand what it is to be surrounded by people who

seem to be wonderfully gifted in the work that the Lord has called them to do. They just seem so wise and strategic. Or they seem to see things in Scripture that I have not seen and then preach so magnificently. I have, in my younger years, tried to copy them, but it was usually ineffective. The Lord had not told me to copy them, but to be who I am in Him.

To try and copy someone else in ministry is like David trying to fight in King Saul's armour. It just does not work. David could not function in the wonderful armour that Saul had. Instead, he went as he was, with no armour and used his sling and some stones. It seems strange to us. He seemed to be so ill-equipped to fight a giant. Yet, he was walking in the gifting and training that God has formed in him over the hidden years.

Seemingly unconnected encounters with a lion and a bear had trained him for this moment. His life up until now had been the moulding ground the Lord had used for this encounter. He didn't try to copy anyone else. He just walked in the gifting that God has given him. Do not try to be someone else. Be who the Lord has formed you to be.

What is Jesus saying to you?

71. UNCLE DAN

Scripture

Now it is God who makes both us and you stand firm in Christ. He anointed us… (2 Corinthians 1:21)

Therefore put on the full armour of God, so that when the day of evil comes, you may be able to stand your ground, and after you have done everything, to stand. (Ephesians 6:13)

And if what was transitory came with glory, how much greater is the glory of that which lasts! (2 Corinthians 3:11)

The Heart of Jesus for you

Jesus says: I know that you think you literally cannot go on any longer, but you can. I created you. I formed you. I empowered you. I know what you can and cannot do, and I know that, with my help, you can continue. I am not asking you to do anything, but stand and that takes courage when you are exhausted and are experiencing disappointment. There is a greater glory waiting for you in the next life. This life is preparing you for a future glory.

As the enemy advances, stand. As exhaustion encroaches, stand. As disappointment seeps in, stand. You are my child and I love you so, so much and I celebrate you. The story of your faith will be told to the generations to come, and they will be inspired by what happened in and through you. Let me fill you now with the Holy Spirit in order that you can stand...

Thought

I can remember Uncle Dan, tall with a shock of white curly hair. He was not my Uncle, but my grandmother's brother-in-law. But, he was family. He had been a prisoner of war and here is a part of his story:

"Quickly the infuriated guards jumped lion-like on their helpless victim, a mere ninety-seven pound shadow of the proud Scottish soldier who was called to the colours a few years previously. I stood there in their midst - I never felt so alone and helpless in my life as at that moment. I stood naked but for my ragged loincloth. Bearded, with hair falling to my shoulders, the flesh had almost disappeared from my tall six-foot frame. Hollow eyes and cheeks, collapsed abdomen, pitifully thin legs and arms, I stood feeling utterly helpless… Instantly I received strength, and the mysterious consciousness of the Divine Presence of my blessed Saviour permeated my whole being. Humanly speaking, I was at the point of no return. None of my comrades dared to help me in the face of this ruthless and bloodthirsty enemy. But instantaneously and gloriously my fears completely left me.

To the four Japanese guards I must have seemed easy prey as I stood there utterly helpless. They huddled together for a conference. Breaking away, they jumped around me briefly, screaming with rage. Then they struck; swift and sure came the cruel blows, each one a killer. With feet and fist they pummelled my weak frame until I crumpled at their feet beaten into insensibility. Throwing a bucket of cold water over me brought me back to consciousness, where I was hauled to my feet by determined assailants. Through misty eyes I could see them stealthily advancing upon me again. Suddenly the blows began to fall on my weakened frame. I tried to resist them but they came from all directions; unmercifully and relentlessly they fell, then semi-consciousness faded into total darkness and relief.

Being brought back to consciousness for the second time, I felt that I was living my last few moments on Earth...Thus fortified, the inner peace and radiance burst through the filth, the scars and the coagulated blood, and formed a smile -- the onlookers said that it was a Heavenly smile. The furious Japanese soldiers stared in disbelief; there was some Power here, which they had never encountered before and could not understand. How could one endure such punishment and be so close to death, and smile? They were incensed to the point of insanity. No puny, filthy prisoner would mock their disciplinary action...From thirty feet away they advanced on their helpless prey. Terrified and helpless fellow prisoners stood around. They had witnessed and heard the sickening thud of each death-dealing blow... On came the rushing soldiers, murder in their hearts, shrieking and yelling as they ran -- twelve feet, ten feet, eight feet, seven, six, five, four. Suddenly those baffled men skidded to a stop. They looked incredulously at each other and stared with amazement at this battered and bloody archenemy. They retreated slowly to their former position to review their strategy. They worked themselves up into a frenzy; they yelled and screamed and waved their arms around as they began their advance on their seemingly forlorn victim. Could the truth have been known I was never stronger than at that moment of human weakness...While breathless buddies watched, I waited -- physically weak but never more strong. Onward rushed the guards, bent on ending this sordid affair. Twelve feet, eight, six, four. Again around the three-foot mark they skidded to a stop, as though facing an invincible barrier, which they could not penetrate. Now utterly baffled and confused they stared at each other in disbelief. They were obviously bewildered... What drove them to distraction was the look of serenity, or was it a look of triumph? Then there was this unseen Presence, the irresistible Power, and the invisible Hedge: they were baffled and perplexed... They could find no solution to any of their immediate problems and in utter dismay and disgust they retreated into the bamboo jungle. I could hardly believe that my accusers had left, yet was not surprised, for in the days prior to my enlistment the Lord had given me the precious promise, "I will never leave thee nor forsake thee."[16]

What is Jesus saying to you?

---

[16] http://plymouthbrethren.org/author/13 - Daniel Snadden

72. WIN/WIN

Scripture

For to me, to live is Christ and to die is gain.
(Philippians 1:21)

Stand firm, and you will win life. (Luke 21:19)

Brothers and sisters, I do not consider myself yet to
have taken hold of it. But one thing I do: Forgetting what is
behind and straining toward what is ahead, I press on
toward the goal to win the prize for which God has called
me Heavenward in Christ Jesus. (Philippians 3:13-14)

The Heart of Jesus for You

Jesus says: You are in a win-win scenario. You cannot
lose, unless you turn your back on me. I know that you
won't do that. You have me in life and you gain more of
me in death. That is the good news of faith. The outcome
is not in doubt. I have defeated the Devil on the cross and
in the resurrection. The victory is secure and I turned what
looked like defeat on the cross into victory in the
resurrection. I am doing that within you. I am turning

defeat into victory. Let me remind you that I have saved you, forgiven you, cleansed you, made you into a new creation, have given you a new heart, have enabled you to enter into the presence of my Father. You are saved for all eternity…

Thought

One of my all time favourite quotes is from the missionary Jim Elliott: "He is no fool who gives what he cannot keep to gain what he cannot lose." It sends shivers over me even just typing it up. In 1956 Jim Elliott was a missionary who went to tell the Huorani people in Ecuador about Jesus. Unfortunately, he and the other four with him with him were killed, as they told people about Jesus. It can feel from our perspective that we can lose. But we can't. Jesus took care of that on the cross. If we live, we have Jesus. If we die, we have more of Jesus. Two years after Jim Elliott and his friends had died, Jim's wife, Elisabeth, their daughter and the sister of one of the missionaries, moved to the village to live among her husbands killers. Many of the tribe became followers of

Jesus. An incredible testimony of love, perseverance and resilience.

The Apostle Paul constantly lived with the threat of being killed for the faith. He did not live from a place of fear, but a place of faith and hope. Let me ask you a question: Do you truly, truly believe that when you die you will be with Jesus? Or is it just a hope? If Heaven is real and we will truly be with Jesus, then why would we be afraid of death? It's been defeated. We will live for eternity. The free gift of Jesus is eternal life. It's all win-win. I don't particularly want to die, but I do truly believe in the life that is waiting for us.

In Mozambique, where we lived for a time, followers of Jesus are being martyred. A machete is put to their necks and they are asked to denounce Jesus. Whole families are put to death because of their faith in Jesus. Pray for them, and pray that we may all have their faith in Jesus.

What is Jesus saying to you?

73. MULTIVERSE

Scripture

Set your minds on things above, not on Earthly things. (Colossians 3:2)

For, as I have often told you before and now tell you again even with tears, many live as enemies of the cross of Christ. Their destiny is destruction, their god is their stomach, and their glory is in their shame. Their mind is set on Earthly things. But our citizenship is in Heaven. And we eagerly await a Saviour from there, the Lord Jesus Christ, who, by the power that enables him to bring everything under his control, will transform our lowly bodies so that they will be like his glorious body. (Philippians 3:18-21)

The Heart of Jesus for You

Jesus says: You are living in two realms at the same time. You are straddling two realities. You physically live in the Earthly realm. You spiritually live in the Heavenly realms, seated with me. You can choose to live and make decisions based on the earthly realm, in which case, you become distant from me in the Heavenly realm. Or, you live from Heavenly places, and let that direct how you live on Earth. You should remain so Heavenly minded that you impact Earth for my glory. If you just live with an Earthly mindset you will live by your body or your emotions and thoughts. If you live from Heavenly places, the Holy Spirit will be your guide and your body and mind will be led by the Holy Spirit. The riches and resources of Heaven are available to you and I am sitting next to you in the Heavenly realms...

Thought

The story of Elisha and his servant illustrates the fact that we live in two realms. They both are surrounded by the army of Aram. The whole city is surrounded. There is no escape. 'When the servant of the man of God got up and went out early the next morning, an army with horses and chariots had surrounded the city. "Oh no, my lord! What shall we do?" the servant asked.' (2 Kings 6:15) The servant's response is usually our response: panic.

Elisha calmly replies: "Don't be afraid," the prophet answered. "Those who are with us are more than those who are with them."

And Elisha prayed, "Open his eyes, LORD, so that he may see." Then the LORD opened the servant's eyes, and he looked and saw the hills full of horses and chariots of fire all around Elisha. (2 Kings 6:16-17). Around you at the moment is a spiritual world that you cannot normally see. Angels are around you. Jesus is with you.

In the story of Shadrach, Meshach and Abednego the supernatural realm is revealed. They are thrown into the fire that has already killed soldiers. Scripture tells us: Then King Nebuchadnezzar leaped to his feet in amazement and asked his advisers, "Weren't there three men that we tied up and threw into the fire?" They replied, "Certainly, Your Majesty." He said, "Look! I see four men walking around in the fire, unbound and unharmed, and the fourth looks like a son of the gods." (Daniel 3:24-25)

There's a fourth man standing in the fire - do not be afraid.

What is Jesus saying to you?

74. FOUNDATION

Scripture

Therefore everyone who hears these words of mine and puts them into practice is like a wise man who built his house on the rock. The rain came down, the streams rose, and the winds blew and beat against that house; yet it did not fall, because it had its foundation on the rock. (Matthew 7:24-25)

...or no one can lay any foundation other than the one already laid, which is Jesus Christ. If anyone builds on this foundation using gold, silver, costly stones, wood, hay or straw, their work will be shown for what it is, because the Day will bring it to light. It will be revealed with fire, and the fire will test the quality of each person's work. If what has been built survives, the builder will receive a reward. If it is burned up, the builder will suffer loss but yet will be saved—even though only as one escaping through the flames. (1 Corinthians 3:11-15)

The Heart of Jesus for You

Jesus says: Check your foundations. On what foundation are you building? It can be so easy to start building on me as a foundation and then start to add other things into the foundation mix because things are not happening fast enough or are not tuning out in the way that you want. Make sure that I am your only foundation. I am the Rock and I am the Chief Cornerstone. Two houses can look identical, but dive deeper into the foundations and you may discover that they are very different. One will last and the other will not. If you have me as your foundation, you will do as I say, no matter what the cost, and you will live in the way I have directed you to live. My ways are the best ways and they will give you life…

Thought

If people have Jesus as their foundation then why do so many crash and burn? Jesus says that if you hear his words and do them, then what is built in your life will be strong and you will not fall when the storms of life come. Many followers not standing, but falling instead. That suggests, according to Scripture, that they are not putting the words of Jesus into practice. So, the way to start to build Jesus as his foundation is to do what he commands. The foundation building starts with obedience. My foundation is Jesus and I will do as he directs. Read the Sermon on the Mount (Matthew 5-7) and see what areas of your life need to alter and make sure that Jesus is the Rock on which you stand. Read the book of James and be challenged to show your faith by what you do.

When we stand before the throne of God, nothing else will matter, apart from how we responded to Jesus. Did we love Him? Did we follow Him? Did we obey His commands? Choose life this day. Choose Jesus. Always.

What is Jesus saying to you?

Printed in Great Britain
by Amazon